Children and their Temperaments

Marieke Anschütz

Children
and their
Temperaments

Floris Books

Translated by Tony Langham and Plym Peters

First published in Dutch under the title *Ons Temperament*
by Uitgeverij Christofoor, Zeist 1991

First published in English by Floris Books in 1995
Reprinted 1999

British Library CIP data available

ISBN 0-86315-175-2

Printed in Great Britain
by Cromwell Press, Trowbridge, Wilts

Contents

1	A question: by way of foreword	7
2	Types and typologies	9
3	A source of confidence	13
4	Back to the origins	19
5	A new formulation of an old concept	26
6	Four in one	30
7	The four temperaments in colour	39
8	Born four times	52
9	Up to the age of fourteen	58
10	After twice seven years	64
11	The number of the earth	69
12	The four Evangelists	74
13	The black square	86
14	Fairy tales as a guide	93
15	Moving mountains	101
16	Seeing the wood through the trees	106
17	Eating what's on the table	113
18	Four children in the class	123
19	In conclusion: an answer	127
	Bibliography	128

– 1 –

A question:
by way of foreword

"It's strange that you never really get to know anyone ..." She was silent for a moment and then went on: "... not even yourself." Her voice sounded meditative and surprised about this discovery and its possible consequences. It was as though she saw the riddle before her in the dark, and was carefully exploring it. That is why it sounded like a question, although it wasn't really framed as one.

——— o Θ o ———

It was evening. My fourteen-year-old daughter was in bed and we were sitting up talking things over. The shaft of light from the landing was enough to make us feel that the darkness was listening to us. This time of day is often good for talking confidentially, not usually about deep secrets, but more about the things that are just hidden below the surface of busy, demanding day-time life. There is a sort of undercurrent of ideas and insights which need an opportunity to be expressed, so that all these "invasions" surface into our conscious minds, if only for a little while.

Often these confidences concern experiences at school with classmates, friends or teachers. Sometimes there is something like that unspoken question above which seems to come from everywhere and nowhere. It was a question which stayed in my mind because it contains a riddle.

Many months later I suddenly came across something like an answer to the riddle ...

– 2 –

Types and typologies

Most people who become involved with a Steiner school through their children, are drawn into the school after a while, not only in a physical way, but also spiritually. What happens at school is so fascinating that they want to know whether it is inspired by God or the Devil. Then we start to take an interest in the background which determines the teacher's activities and lessons. First of all, there is the curriculum which was passed on to teachers by Rudolf Steiner, the founder of anthroposophy, as a guideline for their lessons. Anyone who is interested can read a book on this subject about the lessons covered in every class. In addition, every class has its own theme for the year, and a close look reveals that this is the "golden thread" which runs through everything covered in that particular year. However, all these elements are only a framework, a sort of skeleton which provides a structure and support for the content of the lessons, serves as a guideline for the teacher's ideas, and can be a source of inspiration for anyone who is trying to fill out this framework.

The curriculum and the teacher's work are based on

a philosophy, a particular way of looking at man and the world, known as anthroposophy, or spiritual science. Putting this philosophical method into practice is a task which confronts every teacher, every day. They are concerned not only with the children in their class but also with themselves. When the first Steiner School opened in Stuttgart in 1919, Rudolf Steiner gave a course for the first group of teachers in which he not only discussed and explained parts of the curriculum in great detail, but in addition gave instructions to the teachers about how they should relate to the children and to themselves. He did not achieve this by doing it for them, but by teaching them to see other people, themselves and children in a particular way. Of course, they did not become proficient straightaway, just as any teacher nowadays does not learn how to teach straightaway. Structures and classifications can be learned quickly, and the categories of a curriculum can soon be made familiar, but what matters is that every day we bring to life a small part of that apparently lifeless set of ideas.

In a sense, this special way of looking at people can be learnt by anyone who wants to know what happens in class. Certainly it is good practice for parents to try and understand the lesson content and to live with the concepts which are embodied in school, bringing them into their own situation, the family and their own work, so that they translate them into their own lives. If this is done, and the curriculum is accepted as a working hypothesis, you will see that over the years you gain a better understanding of the aims of the teachers at a

Steiner school. Those who strive to gain insight themselves will also recognize that search in others.

Although Rudolf Steiner was very flexible regarding
the fundamental ideas of anthroposophy and the related
methods and principles for education, and discussed
these from many different perspectives, highlighting
completely new aspects every time, it is better for our
purposes to start with a simple structure so that we
become familiar with certain terms. During teacher
training, students are introduced to a number of different "schools" of psychology and character study.
German, English and French educationalists have all
identified and described different *typologies;* they
divide people into certain types on the basis of their
experience and research. The number of types distinguished varies between systems. The German and
English schools divide people into three types, while
the French school, dating back to the end of the
eighteenth century, distinguishes four types. Students at
the Steiner teacher training college are also taught a
typology, the one used in Steiner schools and which,
like the French school, has four classes. This typology
is meant to inform the educational method practised,
but the teacher achieves this meaningfully only because
the four types are related to the anthroposophical view
of the human being as fourfold. We will return to this
in detail as we go on.

The four types do not have French but Greek names,
and the word used to describe them is "temperaments."
The concept is older than the word itself, because the
Latin word *temperamentum* has been used in this sense

only since the seventeenth century, while the concept goes back more than two thousand years.

It is quite fascinating to follow the development of words. We now use the word "temperament" to mean "mood," or a particular type, as in a "temperamental" person. However, the original meaning of the Latin word is "mixture," in the sense that the interbalance of elements must be right for everything to be in balance. It is a chemical term taken from ancient medicine.

Reading the above, you may wonder why Rudolf Steiner, a philosopher of our time, borrowed these old words in combination with the new insights of his spiritual science. To find out why he did this we will take a look at the historical origins of this ancient medicine and the Greek names for the classification of types which came to be passed on to us in Steiner schools.

– 3 –

A source of confidence

When you begin to study the notion of the four temperaments, you imagine that you are concerned with the field of educational psychology. This is quite correct in so far as the children or adults concerned are normal and healthy. However, when the typology reveals extremes in the form of magnified and exaggerated effects, boundaries become blurred and you soon find yourself entering the field of medicine. This in itself is not very surprising as the doctrine of the temperaments is derived from ancient medicine.

Before studying the question of how and where western medicine originated, and where the temperaments originally came from, I would like to mention two names from the long history of medical science in Europe. I do so for the following reason. The way in which modern medical practitioners speak rather condescendingly about their colleagues from earlier centuries begs a rather puzzling question. If those physicians of yesteryear were unable to perform as much as we can because their knowledge was limited, where did they get the confidence to do their work at all? Why were they not filled with despair when they saw so many people die in their care? Why did they not leave their groaning patients to their fate? Compassion and the desire to help are not sufficient in a case of extreme need. For those physicians of ancient times, there must have been some other source of assurance and strength.

I suspect that we tacitly ignore a whole dimension in medicine that I can only approach by naming two figures, two physicians who gained great international fame in their lifetime, a fame which was incomprehensible from a scientific point of view. They were both great scholars, but there were many such people. Neither of them is well known for any particular discovery in the medical field. No diseases or instruments have been named after them. Therefore there must be another reason for their great fame, above all at a time when communication in Europe was still very slow.

The first person I would mention is Herman Boerhaave (1668–1738), the son of a pastor from a village near Leiden in Holland. He started studying theology and natural philosophy in Leiden and for some time he worked in the university library. Then he decided to devote himself entirely to the study of medicine. Boerhaave never left his own country, the Netherlands; the furthest he ever travelled in his life was a trip to Harderwijk for a few days to obtain his medical degree at the Academy of Gelderland. Degrees were cheaper there. However, he did not have to go into the world; the world soon came to him. Once he had been appointed as a lecturer — and later professor — of theoretical medicine, he proved to be a born teacher. His lectures were collected in two Latin textbooks, which were soon translated and printed throughout Europe. In the meantime he had also become a professor of botany. Boerhaave was responsible for the development of the botanical gardens in Amsterdam, the gardens in the Academy. His students came from all over Europe, and half of the people at his lectures were usually foreign. But it was striking that on a personal level he was a wise counsellor for his students, and the best of these returned to their own countries to organize the academic teaching according to the example they had experienced in Leiden. Boerhaave was known as the "Teacher of Europe," and one anecdote relates that a letter from China addressed only to "Boerhaave — Europe," was eventually delivered to the right address. After his death it became clear how great his personal influence had been, because the fame of Leiden soon waned.

What was the secret of his enormous influence? The secret of Boerhaave was Boerhaave himself. His complete integrity and his universal knowledge, which was based on wisdom and thoughtful critical judgment, were accompanied by very high moral and religious convictions. The strength of his work and life was founded on the true life of a Christian, and his contemporaries recognized this in him. Perhaps that is why he recommended the study of Hippocrates, the forefather of medicine, in his inaugural speech as a lecturer. On the basis of his deeply religious convictions he saw something in the works of this ancient wise Greek which his colleagues could no longer see. The Hippocratic oath was considered to be out of date.

The second great individual I would like to name is Maimonides. He was a Spanish physician in the twelfth century and was very celebrated in his own time. One of his morning prayers has survived and its very simplicity provides the answer to the question about the source of his strength to continue his work as a doctor day after day. It is permeated with a wisdom and humility which every modern doctor could benefit from.

The morning prayer
Stand by me, Almighty Father, in performing my difficult task so that it will succeed, because without your support man is not capable of the slightest thing. Fill me with love for my art and your creatures, and do not allow money or ambition to influence my deeds, because these enemies of truth and the love of mankind could easily lead me to stray from the path and prevent me from my duty to help your children.

Enlarge my heart so that it is always prepared to help the poor and the rich, friends and foes, the evildoers as well as those who do good. Allow me to see only the man in the person who is suffering; give me the strength to command myself by the sick bed so that I do not have any wandering thoughts and all my knowledge and experience is available to help him. Grant my patients the trust in me and in my art so that they will be

confident about following my prescriptions
and instructions.

Grant me, oh God, patience and gentleness
when a sick man opposes me; grant me moderation in everything except in my longing
for knowledge. Grant me modesty so that I
do not have any arrogant ideas about my
skills. Gird my loins with armour when igno-
rant people mock me, so that my mind remains untainted and continues to seek truth,
despite other influences. However, if wiser
men wish to teach me more, let my mind be
grateful to follow the path shown, because
the field of medicine is very large. Amen.

There are signs that the arrogance of modern science
no longer convinces everyone. A recent history of
medical science in the Netherlands cautiously suggests
that, in addition to the technical and mechanical aspects
of illness, there is also a side which confronts most
doctors, though many do not know what to do with it.
I quote from the concluding chapter:

The scientific and technical development of
medicine continues to progress and medical
knowledge is constantly growing. Therefore
we could simply write about the development
of medical science seen as a pure science.
But it happens to be the case that man can be
said to consist of a body and a soul ...

In more than half the cases they deal with,

doctors are confronted with symptoms and complaints which they cannot account for in purely organic scientific terms. Even the ancient Greeks who followed in the footsteps of Hippocrates knew that the human being must be considered as a whole, with both physical and spiritual qualities, when forming the prognosis of an illness.

The author ends rather sadly: "To understand the spiritual background is always more difficult." These words are beside a photograph of an operation in a modern teaching hospital. It is hard to imagine a clearer image for the situation in which humanity now finds itself. For a modern doctor, the source of strength and confidence lies in the physical and sensory world — as least as long as this lasts.

– 4 –

Back to the origins

For the ancient Greeks, the world of the senses and perceptions was closely related to the invisible world — the divine and spiritual world. The former was a direct expression of the latter. This link, which was a self-evident truth for the ancient Greeks, can only be conceived of in images by us.

Modern medicine has retained a few vestiges of these early times: the Hippocratic Oath, though this is no longer taken in its original form, and the scalpel, the distinguishing mark of a physician's profession. The name of this sign was taken from Asklepios (in Latin: Aesculapius).

In Greek mythology, Asklepios was described as the son of the Sun God, Apollo, and a mortal mother, Coronis, the daughter of the King of Thessalonica. She was unfaithful to her lover, and the angry god ordered his sister Artemis to shoot her infallible arrows at her. When the grieving royal parents placed their dead daughter on the funeral pyre, Apollo had second thoughts and saved his small son from the burning body of his mother.

Asklepios grew up on Mount Pelion, raised by the centaur Chiron, who taught the boy the secrets of nature. Asklepios became the great healer of the sick and there are remains throughout Greece of the holy places devoted to this "saviour." Although these were also places of mystery, and initiates had to keep silent about them, a few stories nevertheless were handed down, such as the account of the words over the entrance of the temple to Asklepios in Epidaurus:

> Let anyone who enters in the temple,
> Fragrant with incense, be pure.
> Pure means:
> To move the divine in a thoughtful mood.

We know that the body and soul are interrelated. But in ancient Greek culture this was seen in such a way that a pure soul was a precondition for healing the body. In the Greek mind the body became sick when the soul shut itself off from the divine world. Therapy was only used once the soul had been purified, which means it had been reunited with the divine world. The ancient Greeks knew this reinforced the regenerative strength of the body. Healing was a religious matter and therefore the purification of the soul was a precondition.

Epidaurus is a very sorry place and almost no stones are left standing. The only thing which has more or less survived intact is the theatre, which lies in the hills like a great conch shell. This was the place where the soul was purified, where the sick underwent a catharsis and where the Mystery plays were performed. In ancient times there was an altar in the centre of the circular stage, the orchestra. I once saw a performance of the tragedy *Antigone* by Euripides in a suburb of Athens. The play was excellently performed by amateurs one Sunday afternoon in a small amphitheatre built in the classical style. In the centre of the stage there was a rectangular table or tall chest covered with dark cloths. It looked rather like the original altar.

In the ancient theatre of Epidaurus, the image of a huge listening ear becomes even stronger when you stand in the place where the altar was in ancient times and recite a few words: a poem, or some lines from Homer's *Odyssey,* if you have a copy to hand. Something very strange happens: it is as though the sound of the voice is transformed and returns amplified. It is no longer your own familiar small voice; it is as though another greater being speaks to you from the periphery and even speaks through you. At that moment you are literally a "person," a word derived from the Latin *personare,* meaning "to sound through." The ancient players in the Mystery plays wore masks and tall boots because they did not perform as humans, but as *personae* through which the divine could sound.

The theatre where the Mystery plays were held was sometimes called: the ear of Dionysos, the god who worked in the inner regions of man. The devout words spoken at the altar acquired a divine dimension because of the amplification of the sound.

———— o Θ o ————

In an ancient surgery in Enkhuizen, part of a museum open to visitors, you can see a cupboard where a human skeleton was kept in the past for the benefit of medical science. Three figures are painted on the cupboard doors. On the left is a man wearing a cloak trimmed with fur, and a wide-brimmed fur hat. In large letters above his head, you read the name HIPPOCRATES. The man on the right wears the long tunic of a scholar. His dark hair is uncovered and his dark beard descends right down to an open book, where he is pointing out the drawings of herbs. The scholar's name is shown above his head: GALENUS. Between the two figures is a skeleton with its bony hand on its side and, above the bare skull, the inscription: MORS ULTIMA LINEA RERUM ("Death is the extreme limit of things.")

The history of western medicine starts with Hippocrates of Kos (460–377 BC). There was an Asklepios sanctuary on the island of Kos, but at the time that Hippocrates lived the importance of the Mysteries had declined and the knowledge of the priests as healers was becoming discredited. The time seemed right for a new, scientific approach to medicine. Hippocrates was the one who consciously endeavoured to remove the art of healing from the religious sphere and treat it as an independent science. He recorded and catalogued the data of his practice. In countless books this founder of medicine left his records of diagnoses and therapies and these books long served as the basis of the theory of medicine. So the profession of physician came to be established independently of religious authority.

Many centuries later, ancient Rome learnt about the scientific approach to medicine from Greece, which it had conquered. During the second century AD the physician Galen, from Pergamum, visited the Apennine peninsula. He drew up a more or less complete system of the workings of the human body. With regard to the temperaments he related these to the so-called "humours," the bodily fluids. The temperaments derived their names from these:

sanguine	sanguine	blood
phlegmatic	phlegma	mucus
choleric	chole	gall
melancholic	melanchole	black bile

A student of the temperaments will also come across the name of Empedocles (490–430 BC), who was born in Akragas (Agrigentum), a Greek colony on Sicily, and was the founder of the doctrine of the elements. The creation and decay of things, as well as their transformation, is related to the connection or division of earth, water, air and fire. In time the various principles from different philosophical systems were combined in a single powerful structure which survived for thirteen centuries. Galen was the great authority in this field in Europe.

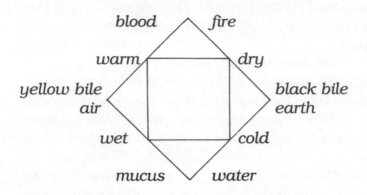

The pharmacists who prepared herbal remedies and made powders and pills were familiar with the system used by physicians when they made their medicines.

The opposing qualities — hot and cold, wet and dry — which are shown in the above system, are derived from the other great founder of this scientific structure: Aristotle (384–322 BC), born at Stagira, a town on the peninsula of Chalcidice, and one of Plato's pupils in Athens. In 343 BC he was ordered by King Philip of Macedonia to educate the young crown prince Alexander, who was later to rule over a vast empire as Alexander the Great.

Finally, the physician Paracelsus (1495–1541) added a new principle to the four elements, the so-called *quinta essentia*. This mysterious fifth element connected the other four and maintained their equilibrium. Every illness has its own "quintessence," and it is an art to find this so that healing can take place.

Since then centuries of research and treatment have

transformed medicine. Medical science is now highly advanced in so many ways, yet an individual who is sick can increasingly feel lost amidst all the impressive medical surroundings. The human body is the focal point of investigation and treatment, to a greater or lesser degree of complexity. The fact that this body is inhabited, governed and formed by a soul and a spirit is something which our medical ancestors undoubtedly knew more about. It may be that Rudolf Steiner took up the old terms for the temperaments because they were meaningful names. He has given them a new content but through their nomenclature they remain linked with their origin: the Mysteries of ancient Greece.

– 5 –

A new formulation of an old concept

Every person has his own temperament. We saw how this was viewed in the past. Scholars related the temperament to the bodily fluids. How can we view this in our own time? Where exactly is the temperament located within the organization of man as a whole? On the one hand, it is something individual, while on the other, it is related to man's general nature, which makes him one of a group.

The temperament seems to stand between two aspects of a person. We are very familiar with these two aspects of ourselves: firstly, the inheritance from parents and ancestors; and secondly, those things which we know we do not share with anyone — the individual, the indivisible aspect. The latter has a basis which is unrelated to the qualities we have inherited in the structure of our bodies. Over and above the development of the species which we have in common with animals, there is the characteristic human development of the individual.

Life on earth is a complete event in itself. But we

would be fooling ourselves if we maintained that our deepest core is already perfect. It looks as though more and more people are prepared to accept the idea that this profound core needs more time to develop than one human life. In one of his lectures Rudolf Steiner stated hopefully: "There will be a time when people will think it is ridiculous that man lives only once and that nothing permanent survives which links a previous existence to the current of inheritance." Sometimes I think that this time has come.

Every person is born with a whole range of characteristics. We could imagine that those characteristics brought with us into the world at birth might conflict with the characteristics of the body that we inherit. How can these two aspects relate when they differ in a fundamental way? Every one of us has these two aspects, with the tension between them. On the one hand, the individual wishes to manifest himself; while on the other, he must adapt to the laws of inheritance. Basically, man's individual essence does not have anything in common with that inheritance. So how is the relationship brought about?

We all know the experience of being invited to a strange place for the first time. We want to go, but we don't know anyone there. In those circumstances, it is very pleasant to be welcomed when we arrive. The person who is host can help to form the link between us and the new environment. I imagine that there is an analogous sort of "host," who creates the connections between our own deepest essential core and the place where we end up in a family, race, or nation with our inherited qualities. This host is what we mean by "temperament."

A careful examination of this function of a "liaison officer" between two worlds shows that it must have been present even before birth. Rudolf Steiner described it as a "careful searching mood" which a person adopts so that his essence can adapt as well as possible to the inherited surroundings when it descends. This adaptation is an ability with which he is born and permeates the inherited substance as a spiritual force.

This could be put in a different way: when two currents collide, there is turbulence. Further on, the river flows on in one stream and the water regains its equilibrium. In the same way, the temperament restores an equilibrium between the eternal and the transient aspects in man.

In a family with a number of children there are obvious differences between the children from the earliest years. And yet they all have the same inheritance and are all brought up in the same environment, so that certain characteristics and physical qualities may become characteristic of all the members of that family.

This applies until the age of seven. When the milk teeth are lost and are replaced by permanent teeth, most children also reveal their own individuality — some more clearly than others. Just as the physical body was liberated from the mother's physical body at birth, the child's etheric body now separates away from the surrounding etheric world. It has fulfilled its task, which is to transform the inherited body into its own individual body. The second set of teeth is the hard physical manifestation in the physical body; that is why it is like the conclusion of the development of an entirely new individual body.

At about the age of fourteen the process of individualization extends to the inner body, the spiritual area. Parents can sometimes be surprised to see how much children change during this period, both outwardly, and above all, inwardly. Sometimes this change is so great that the former child can no longer be recognized. Responses to impressions from outside become more individual or adapt themselves entirely to what the "group" wants.

These are often exciting and worrying years for parents because it seems as though a great deal of what these young people "learned at home" has been forgotten or disappeared into a bottomless well. When the Self is born in the twenties, and separates to develop, all the side roads and alleyways or dead-ends are first explored so that the autonomous individual can test the limits of his being on every side. I think it is by about the age of forty that outsiders can no longer see us as members of one original family. What has happened? Because of the effect of the temperament, part of the inherited substance has become individualized or transformed. This is why, in the course of their lives, children from one family seem to come from that family to a lesser and lesser extent.

– 6 –

Four in one

When we look at an adult as a whole, four "bodies" can be distinguished in accordance with the ideas of anthroposophical spiritual science. This word "body" is taken from the physical world because it is a useful term and relates to an organic whole with specific functions. In the first place, there is the *physical body,* which is an easy point of reference for us. The paradox is that we can only see the bodies which cannot be perceived with the senses, because of the physical body. The way in which our body speaks, moves, and sees, and its overall structure, all enable us to apprehend the other bodies.

The invisible part which is most closely related to the *physical body,* and whose characteristics are also determined by inheritance, is known as the *etheric body* or the *life-force body.* It built up the physical body, and in this sense it is more real than the body which is perceptibly present. Without this etheric body our physical body would fall apart, as in death. When this happens, the etheric body withdraws.

The third body comprises everything which is desired, including feelings of pain and joy, sympathy and antipathy, the instincts as well as ideas and ideals, morality and imagination. It is close to our essential core, our individual deepest Self. In anthroposophical science this aspect is called the *astral body*. In one of his lectures on the four aspects of man Rudolf Steiner wrote: "It is this body which carries desires and drives, that is not the result of the physical body, but its cause." The causal force does not come from the physical world, but from the spiritual world. This thinking based on the spirit is a challenge for us as people of today, because we tend to seek support in material things as a matter of course.

The aspect of the human being which provides the force for self-consciousness is the fourth essential aspect, the bearer of our Self. We can think about ourselves, we can stand back from ourselves and we are able to observe the Self of someone else. When this is no longer the case, when we are no longer able to encounter the Self of another, as happens to some psychiatric patients, this is a very alienating experience. It is not proof that the Self is no longer there.

Bernlef's book, *Hersenschimmen,* describes the disturbed communication between a person suffering from dementia and his environment. It is a fascinating perspective: the spiritual decline is described by the protagonist himself as though the author wishes to indicate that the deepest essence of the person is always there, even when it becomes inaccessible to others. Ideas about the present and the past become confused, and for this person they become equally real. Later on the images are even more fragmented, and the consciousness of the Self recedes further and further, so that he is no longer even affected by the alienated responses from the surrounding world. When we cannot relate any more to the supersensible parts of the human being, we become aware that, although inaccessible to us, they are a reality. And yet we can conclude from this that we can "see" more than we normally think.

The four aspects of the human being — the physical body, the etheric body, the astral body and the Self — are constantly interacting. This is self-evident because, after all, each of us is an indivisible individual, and careful observation enables us to distinguish the four essential aspects of our being, though they can never be separated. Every "body" expresses itself in a way that is characteristic of that body.

This "expression" can be understood in very concrete terms: according to anthroposophy, each of the three immaterial aspects has its own area of influence in the physical body, in which it can function directly and materially. For example, the etheric body expresses itself in the glandular and lymphatic system, the astral body in the nervous and sensory system and the Self in the warmth of the blood.

Working from the basis of these specific influences, we can imagine four types of people:

— in the first type "the blood tends to boil quickly." They "easily get heated" about certain things, and will "go through fire" for things;
— the second behave as though there is a constant

burden on their shoulders and lead in their
shoes, and their body is in their way;

— the third type seem to see, hear, smell and per-
ceive everything, preferably all at once; they
rush into things and have a hundred ideas, of
which less than half are ever fulfilled. They
make contact very easily and let go equally
quickly;

— the fourth type sit down quietly, take their time
for everything they say and do, and will on no
account be hurried, but you can count on them.

In each of these four types of people a particular aspect
is dominant; that is, it colours everything that person
does in a particular way. This is the characteristic
feature of the temperaments. If one of the four aspects
is dominant, this determines the basis of our character,
how we approach the world, how we relate to others
and to ourselves, how we act in difficult situations,
how quickly or how slowly, how superficially or how
thoroughly.

Rudolf Steiner's particular insight was that he saw
the relationship between the different essential aspects
of the human being and the specific colour of each
temperament. This means that the doctrine of the
temperaments acquired a new basis, namely, the
relationship with the four essential aspects of our
being, instead of the ancient doctrine of bodily fluids.
This also enables us to get to know ourselves better in
the difficult field of the temperaments. All of us have
all the four essential aspects within us, but when a

particular aspect predominates we must recognize that this is a manifestation of our individual temperament. The particular colour of this temperament depends on the individual. One melancholic person is not like another.

This can be summarized as follows:

— if *Self-consciousness* dominates in a person, this results in a *choleric* temperament;
— if the influence of the *astral body* is strongest, this means that the person will have a *sanguine* temperament;
— if the *life-force body* predominates in a person, this results in a *phlegmatic* type;
— the *melancholic* temperament is determined by the predominating influence of the *physical* body.

Thus the ancient Greek doctrine of the temperaments has changed in that the four types have a new basis.

In daily life, in the relationship with other people, it is easy to make a mistake about a mood or frame of mind and a person's temperament. A "depressed mood" can be interpreted as a "bad mood," but this does not always have to be the case. Someone with a melancholic temperament has a fairly sombre mood anyway, and his character tends to be more introverted. It would be wrong to interpret his behaviour as a sign of a "bad mood."

Our mood is a matter of light and dark, of being overcast or a bright sky, of rain and sun. A mood has a transient nature, in contrast with our temperament, which is permanent. As we become older and wiser we become better able to control our moods. A child lives in moods and is also extremely sensitive to the moods in his environment. An adult person is expected to learn to "overcome" his moods and to do the work that has to be done, irrespective of his mood. This means that some spontaneity is lost, and is replaced by equilibrium.

It is much more difficult to gain control of our temperament. Our mood, the passing atmosphere, is determined by the weather, by a situation, by physical pain, and is therefore dependent on external circumstances. Our temperament is interrelated to our whole way of being. It is determined from the inside and is therefore much more difficult to "monitor."

Certainly the ideas of spiritual science will show us to be careful about exclamations such as: "What a choleric character he is," which contains an element of criticism. We are all too ready to make moral judgments. On the other hand, it is possible for a temperament to manifest itself in a very one-sided way, and in this case we tend to caricature it. In an adult person this can have a liberating effect if the person concerned can laugh and learn about himself. However, where children are concerned it is important to avoid any tendency to caricature wherever possible.

A negative view of a temperament is not good, for it denies any development and therefore conflicts with our role and task as educators. All Rudolf Steiner's ideas in this field were aimed not at suppressing the dominant temperament, but at helping it to develop in a positive way. The golden rule in relating to children is to accept their temperament for what it is, and work on the basis of that temperament. Our temperament is not a weakness but an opportunity, and determines our potential.

Every temperament has its light and its dark aspects, which means that specific characteristics function positively in certain areas, while they can have a negative effect on the development as a whole because of their one-sided nature. It is an art to use the different temperaments in the right way so that they benefit both the child and society. A positive view of the temperament results in social acceptance and often helps to deal with it in the right way.

A melancholic child does not benefit from exuberant merriment. He may be miserable, but he should learn to direct this towards commiserating with the destiny of other people. The choleric's desire to lead can be directed along the right path if it is used in the correct way. Once the good habits have been learned thoroughly, the loyalty of a phlegmatic person can serve as a support on which we can build. And as for the untidy, fluttering sanguine person who can be so irritating — he can stimulate us outwardly, when we are in danger of getting into a rut. How we would miss his radiant smile, his jokes and his good mood if he weren't there to cheer us up.

With regard to adults, it could be said that anyone who perceives himself as he perceives others will be better able to transform the difficult aspects of his own temperament to become a more balanced person. This takes a whole lifetime and new opportunities arise every day.

───── o Θ o ─────

In the National Gallery in London there is a painting by Hieronymus Bosch, the sixteenth century Dutch painter. The painting is called *The Crowning with Thorns,* referring to the episode recorded in St Matthew's Gospel:

> The soldiers of the Governor took Jesus into the praetorium, and they gathered the whole battalion before him. And they stripped him, and put a scarlet robe on him, and plaiting a crown of thorns, they put it on his head, and put a reed in his right hand. And kneeling before him, they mocked him, saying: "Hail, King of the Jews." (27:28).

The painter has painted this scene with great economy. There is no background, and the large crowd of people is reduced to four figures standing around the One in the middle. These are four splendid characters, four different types who all focus their gaze on the central figure. Their eyes are lit up with greed and there is greed in the despairing lines around their mouths and in the gestures of their grasping hands. One is wearing an iron glove and one holds the crown of thorns threateningly above the prisoner's head; the second grabs hold of the white garment with both hands at the level of the prisoner's heart. The third places his right hand on the prisoner's bound hand, and the fourth comes up to him from behind, placing his hand heavily on the prisoner's shoulder.

The figure in the middle looks at us from Self to Self. It is almost impossible to avoid his eyes. They are the focal point of the painting. Our gaze is constantly drawn back to these eyes. It is as though the painter wishes to say that our central point can be besieged in four different ways, via the head, the heart, the hand and the Self.

These surrounding figures appear to be the shadow sides of the four aspects of the human being and also of the four temperaments, darkened with selfishness. The grasping hands bear witness to this. We have all these four aspects within us, but if we allow that One to enter into the middle, it is possible to achieve a balance.

– 7 –

The four temperaments
in colour

When a well-known film star wanted to play the part
of an autistic character, for many months he studied the
habits, the tics, the customs and the lifestyle and the
ways in which autistic people speak and move. When
he eventually played the part, he seemed to have
incorporated not just a few, but all the characteristics
and idiosyncratic behaviour patterns of a group of
autistic people. It was very clever, but he produced the
image of a person who does not actually exist.

When we describe a temperament we are doing the
same sort of thing. We collect together all the possible
typical characteristics of a particular temperament, but
in practice these are never found all at once in a single
person. Therefore these descriptions can be used as a
guideline for a study, but cannot justify our conclusions. Anyone who uses the doctrine of temperaments
in a practical way refers to it as a working hypothesis:
he uses it as long as the practical situation does not
require any revision. It is only in this way that it is
possible to continue the study and gain a deeper
understanding.

Dick Crum, who has made a thorough study of the temperaments, described an anthroposophical view of them in a series of three published articles. In the first of these, he surveyed the four temperaments and their relationship to the four essential aspects of man:

> When the Self is dominant in the four essen-
> tial aspects, this results in a choleric tempera-
> ment. This predominant aspect of the Self
> primarily has a controlling and consolidating
> effect on the soul, and gives direction. It can
> also have an effect in the physical body,
> which often has a certain dynamic compact-
> ness, with fast, decisive gestures. In general
> the powerful Self in the soul evokes a pro-
> nounced dynamic effect in relation to the
> environment, by means of strong emotions
> and a strong will. It is particularly when this
> is accompanied by a need for manifesting the
> will that there may be a clear manifestation
> of the flow and pulsing of the blood, particu-
> larly in the limbs. This relationship is so
> striking that it is almost always an indication
> of a choleric temperament.
>   The dominant influence of the Self is also
> apparent in a social sense. The central posi-
> tion of the Self in the soul manifests itself in
> a basic attitude in which there is a need to
> become the focal point of a group or commu-
> nity, and to lead it. In many cases the person
> concerned also has a sense of being essential

and will energetically endeavour to realize his own ideas and solutions. The Self is always expressed in a great drive to work and initiative, but it is often inclined to overvalue its own insights and therefore overestimate its own capabilities. Of course, there is a great deal more to say about the relationship of the Self with the choleric temperament than we have briefly indicated here. We are not really concerned with a complete summary of the characteristics of a choleric person, but merely with giving some indication of the person in which the relationship of the essential dominating aspects to the temperament can be interpreted.

When the astral body is dominant, the sanguine temperament emerges. Again there is a clear relationship with the physical body. Just as the Self is linked with the circulation of the blood, the astral body is linked to the nervous and sensory systems. This means that external and internal perception, as well as moods and the entire relationship to the environment, are very important for the sanguine temperament.

The astral body has a very mobile, dynamic nature. This dynamism is changeable and expresses itself in a constant changing of moods, emotions, ideas and impulses of the will, while in addition, there can be rapid changes in the relationship to the environment.

One very striking characteristic of the astral body is the wealth of inner images, both images of the imagination and perceived memories. Therefore the dominance of the astral body leads to an ability to see things inwardly, in clear imaginary sequences, full of colour and movement. In addition, the dynamic and changeable nature of the astral body result in the ability to feel at home almost anywhere, while attention is constantly paid to the specific aspects of any situation.

When the etheric body is dominant, this results in a phlegmatic temperament. In anthroposophy the etheric body is seen as the system of a person's life forces, as the part of his being which builds up the outer form of the physical body and maintains it. After death, when the etheric body has withdrawn from the physical body, physical and chemical processes take place which destroy its physical form. However, during life the etheric body — which is therefore also known as the formative force body — is responsible for the continuity of the external figure. This principle of the continuity of form not only applies in a physical respect, but also determines the basic attitude towards all sorts of situations and events in daily life. For example, when the etheric body is dominant, it gives rise to a need for performing activities in a tried and tested manner, which can de-

velop into a fixed pattern of behaviour. When
this is disrupted by external circumstances, it
often leads to irritation or anxiety after a
while. Therefore, the creation of permanent
habits plays an important role in this temperament. The fact that the life forces are dominant in this case results in a perception of
physical well-being, and this temperament
often seeks situations to reinforce this feeling.
In a physical sense, the system of life forces
often manifests itself in the functioning of
internal secretions and the flow of bodily
fluids. It is known that these move at a much
slower rate than, for example, the circulation
of the blood. When the etheric body dominates the other aspects of a being, it is as
though the person's inner experiences and
events are also subject to this slow movement. The mobility and dynamic nature
which are part of the other aspects of the
being, particularly the Self and the astral
body, are inhibited by this so as to produce
the equanimity, calm and tranquillity of the
phlegmatic temperament.

Finally, the dominance of the physical
body over the other aspects results in a melancholic temperament. In this case the dominance is most clearly expressed in the senses.
Thus, the melancholic person is characterized
by a need to first observe the world, examine
situations independently and see things "with

his own eyes," before he can form his own opinion with any assurance. This is accompanied by a basic approach which reveals itself as a cautious and reserved attitude to new developments, a tendency to detail and careful preparations, and often a certain suspicion towards the environment. The experience of the limitations of the physical body and an awareness of the person's own limited physical potential in relation to the effects of the dangers of the physical environment often results in feelings of impotence, accompanied by an awareness of his own capacities, which are often greatly undervalued.

(Jonas, February/March 1984).

In the next two articles, Dick Crum dealt in more detail with how to view the dominance of the different aspects of a being in concrete terms. This is — and will always be — the basic question for anyone who wishes to work on an anthroposophical basis. In order to be able to recognize the dominant aspect which causes the temperament, it is necessary to review the characteristics of the different aspects of the being. This can be done using practical examples. Crum does it in a very original way by comparing two conflicting temperaments and then assessing them in a specific situation. First, he compares a melancholic with a sanguine temperament. As we have seen, a melancholic person lives strongly through the senses because of the dominance of the physical body, while for a sanguine person perception is particularly important because of the dominance of the astral body. Therefore Crum concludes that in a melancholy person there is virtually no memory of the perceptions which have been seen or heard, while a sanguine person is full of colourful inner images whether these are imaginary or after-images of a perceived reality.

For the two other temperaments, the choleric and phlegmatic, Crum compares the way in which they become angry. Because of the dominance of the etheric body which is characteristic of a phlegmatic person, there is always a strong need for quiet, regularity and a balanced situation. When this situation is disrupted, it always results in irritation. If this does not change, it can lead to an explosion which can surprise onlookers because they are not used to this sort of behaviour from the person concerned. When the Self is dominant the process is different. It is characteristic of a choleric person to feel sure that his own insight into a particular situation is correct, and there is a need to intervene even if his insights are not shared by others. In Crum's words:

> The source of anger in the case of the dominance of the Self rarely or never comes from feelings of irritation, as I described above, but from the fact that the solution to problems which has been aimed at and is considered as the only correct solution, is not seen in the same way by others. This anger can suddenly erupt when a choleric person's efforts to change a situation are not recognized

or valued, or are even opposed. Unlike the phlegmatic temperament, where anger often results in immobility and blocks, the anger resulting from a choleric temperament almost always leads to direct action which fits into a larger strategy and is part of a direct intuitive experience of the situation as a whole.

Finally, Crum comes to the interesting conclusion that a phlegmatic person is inclined to forget unpleasant matters in the course of time, while retaining feelings of rancour, while a choleric person can forgive much more easily without really ever forgetting.

I came across a very good description by Ann Druitt of the temperaments as perceived in children, in *Lifeways*. She compares the characteristics of the temperaments with those of the elements, and characterizes the elements as follows:

Earth
Imagine a rock on a sandy beach, all on its own, shut in itself, hard and cold to the touch, completely immobile and apparently unaffected by what is around it, pressed down by its own weight and slightly sinking down into the ground below ...

Water
Let us begin by looking at a drop of water: smooth, round, perfectly enclosed in itself, a small world in itself ...

Air

Air does not belong to anyone or anything,
but is shared by everyone — air carries all
sounds ..., is constantly in motion and causes
the movements of other things. It has a local-
ized effect, and also easily covers large distances. When it is kept in one place too long
it becomes stuffy and poor; when it is put
under pressure it will probably explode ...

Fire

No one ignores a fire. Everyone is attracted
by the enormity of fire, and people naturally
draw near, possibly grateful for its heat and
light, sometimes full of awe, or simply fascinated by the activity and energy which it
radiates ...

Ann Druitt extends these ideas to the human individual,
and interrelates them in corresponding images. Here are
some of her descriptions of children:

The melancholic child

A rock speaks to us about the distant past,
and a melancholic child sometimes looks like
a "little old man" or "rather old-fashioned
little girl." The child has a pale face and a
veiled look as if the eyes — although open to
the world — are gazing inwards. He finds it
difficult to interact harmoniously with others.
This sort of child is often the target of other

children's japes, the victim of practical jokes
which make him deeply unhappy.

The phlegmatic child

A phlegmatic child feels comfortable in his
isolation, ... Water is refreshing, and a phlegmatic child who is socially active is able to
refresh others, to cure them of their sorrows,
to reduce their frustration, to combat their
restlessness and give them a sense of stability
and confidence in the future.

The sanguine child

His ears are open, and catch his name whispered at a distance of a hundred metres, or
hear the noise of paper being rustled three
rooms away. Watching the movements of the
air, as revealed in steam or smoke, we become aware of its complexity and beauty. In
this child there is an artist at work in a flexible, constantly changing form. For parents,
this mobility can be irritating, but it should
be seen as a challenge to avoid ordering the
child to sit still.

The choleric child

Fire flares into life very quickly, and is also
very quickly extinguished. In the fire of his
enthusiasm the choleric child often fails to
take other people's feelings into account, but
when his own soul is wounded, he feels it

deeply, and his inner flame is extinguished.
He always wants the approval and support of
others to give him the warm glow of success.
This is a fuel he needs, not just for fulfilling
the task which he has undertaken — for he
will do this anyway — but to inspire another
project.

What appeals to me in Ann Druitt's description is the
way she reveals the "pros and cons" of a particular
element, and therefore of the temperament which goes
with it. Fire can be destructive, but if it is tempered, it
can radiate a pleasant warmth; water can have a
calming, beneficial effect, but it also has a concealed
tendency towards storms and violence.

The air is the element available for everyone, and
full of movement, but it is precisely because of its
volatility that it may not provide a stable base in the
earth. The earth itself is the element of the melancholic
child — earth, permanence, self-sufficiency — but it
also has the beauty and variety of the mineral world.
We often think that rocks and stones have something
to hide.

I shall never forget a walk I had on the east coast of
Scotland. We were looking for stones which were said
to contain hidden agates. As long as the stones remained closed, we could imagine that they contained
the most beautiful crystals. When they were split open,
it was usually a disappointment. But that was merely
because we had not searched properly.

In this way the temperaments colour the windows of

our soul. When the sun of our personality shines through, it becomes clear whether there is harmony in the palette of colours. This harmony can be achieved only when we realize that the dominant temperament is one-sided, and that we need the other temperaments to supplement our own.

Obviously there is much more to say about this, and there are many questions which remain, for example:

— Why am I lumbered with this temperament?
— Was I given this temperament, or did I choose it?
— Is it a matter of fate ?
— Why am I like I am?

Anyone who studies the temperaments will come up against these questions, to their irritation, despair or astonishment. If you allow the world before birth, which includes the world of the dead, to enter into your thoughts, you will probably get a lot further.

A preacher in Amsterdam, Anne de Graaf, wrote in a newspaper article *(Trouw,* May 1983) that social workers often find it difficult to identify their clients' questions as existential questions. She believes that this is partly due to the fact that "matters of faith" are not described as they were in the past in the images and words of the traditional Church:

> Raising questions about the meaning of life is not a prerogative of the Church, which has — often through its own fault — been pushed to the periphery of society. Helpers who think

that they can refer such questions, when raised by their clients, to a Church body, or who consider that special qualifications are needed to respond at this level, fail to recognize the central role which these questions play in the healing process of those who turn to them. The energy to work on the problem which gave rise to the request for help often returns only when attention is also focussed on questions about the deeper meaning of life and "matters of faith."

In view of the origin of the temperaments, which arise from a therapeutic religious context, the understanding expressed here connects with that founding insight across the centuries.

52

– 8 –

Born four times

A friend had come home with my daughter from school, a tall, almost skinny girl with a long narrow face and straight fair hair. Her narrow shoulders were slightly hunched as though she was carrying an invisible weight. Her large dark eyes made her white face look even narrower. She did not make any unnecessary movements. They went upstairs. In the bedroom there was a large wooden box, the front of which had been sawn away. The box had been changed into a shop. The shelves were full of groceries and there were pots and bottles and boxes everywhere. The customers came in and rang a real bell. There were little bags hanging on a wire ready to wrap up the groceries. Our children often played with this. They had even made some money to pay with. The friend stayed in the middle of the room and looked quietly at the shop, her arms hanging down by her side. She looked at the counter, a block of wood painted brown, and at the nice little copper scales. Then she said to the girls who had shown it to her: "Show me how to play with it."

The child described here is so clearly handicapped by her melancholic temperament, we could almost pity her. In children, a particular temperament can often be perceived with such clear outlines that it seems the child has put on that particular "coat." It is as though the temperament is almost stuck on to the child from outside and is not determined from the inside, as in an adult.

This observation can give rise to the question whether a temperament is different for children than it is for adults. There is something mysterious about a child's temperament, something intangible. Many teachers think that they know their children and yet are constantly surprised. In practice it becomes clear that the obvious aspect of a child's temperament is often an illusion. Often a child will show a totally different side of himself at home from the side that he shows at school.

In 1908 and 1909, Rudolf Steiner, the founder of anthroposophy, gave lectures on the temperaments. Ten years later when the first Steiner school was founded, the same theme returned in his educational lectures for teachers. However, there was one important difference: in the first three lectures the temperaments were described as they appear in adults. In 1919, Steiner concluded that it was different for children.

A few years ago an article by Wolfgang Schad appeared in the *Lehrer Rundbrief* (1982, no. 21), in which he described the background to Rudolf Steiner's conclusion in some detail. When Steiner expressed his views on the temperaments and described how these are an extension of the four essential aspects of a person, he did so on the basis of the situation for an adult. The temperament of a child should not and cannot be judged on the basis of the adult situation, because the basis of the temperaments — the four aspects of the person — are still veiled in a child and are only "born" over the course of many years. If it is assumed that the relationship between these essential aspects and the temperaments also applies to children, the difficulties which a teacher encounters when he is classifying temperaments in his class, are of a different level. Before we look more closely at Wolfgang Schad's explanation, it is a good idea to take another look at this "birth" of the essential aspects of a person.

The four essential aspects which determine the temperament are fully present in an adult. In a child they are still concealed. It is as though they are wrapped up and have to be unwrapped. We could also say that a person has to be born four times before he is able to enter into adulthood.

The first birth — that of the *physical body* — requires about forty weeks of preparation. When this body is separated it is ready in so far as it can now be transformed. Parents and carers are responsible for the physical conditions and influences. It is very important to see how we influence the various senses, for example the sense of touch, by the choice of materials, clothes and toys which a child is given. As parents, we can help him to build his own "house" for this inherited body in the first seven years by means of the food, environment, stories and the religious background we provide. This is also the period in which the etheric body is being formed.

When the second set of permanent teeth start to come through, the *etheric* body is born, ready to be formed during the stage that the child is still a young schoolchild. During this stage the teacher has a very important function. Everything in the world enters the child through the teacher. At this time it is often the teacher's task to bring everything, even the most ordinary things, to the children in images, not only in a physical and perceptual way, but particularly from a spiritual point of view.

> The authority which is accepted as being self-evident and is not enforced must be an immediate image for the youngster's experience from which he develops his conscience, his habits and his tendencies. The temperament develops in accordance with this and these are the eyes through which the child sees the world. Respect and awe are forces which help to develop the etheric body in the right way. Anyone who has not had the opportunity to look at someone with boundless respect during this particular period of development will pay for it for the rest of his life. If this respect is lacking, the living forces of the etheric body suffer.
> (Rudolf Steiner, *The Education of the Child.*)

This is also the ideal time to train the memory.

With the onset of puberty the *astral body* is born with many labour pains before and after the birth. The youngster is now physically able to produce a being of his own sort. But his Self is still being developed. Anyone who spends time with young people of this age can become irritated by their arrogant tone, full of exaggerated egotism, which is not matched by a comparable sense of responsibility. But a teacher should not really expect this: it is understandable that in most youngsters at this stage of development, while the emerging sense of responsibility should be practised, it is not yet fully established.

In order to communicate from Self to Self, the child's *own Self* must be developed. However, this is not born until about the age of twenty-one. This essential aspect of a person is not yet finished at that stage; it takes at least seven years for the Self to develop fully. It is one of the most frustrating experiences in modern society that there is no space, or very little space for young people to develop their Self in their twenties, to deal with old experiences and go through new unprogrammed experiences, that is, in order to learn about people and experience life. In an ideal world, all youngsters coming to the end of a long formal school education should go out into the wide world to do meaningful work and learn to know themselves.

In addition, we increasingly see that young people are asked to give an opinion about matters on which it is impossible for them to have a view, in conflict with the constant paternalism they experience from above.

The critical faculties should have an opportunity to develop and mature in complete peace and tranquillity, on the basis of many different experiences, just as the unborn child develops in the mother's womb without any direct influence from outside.

We saw that many people who work with children raise the question whether a child's temperament is different from that of an adult. As we may assume the essential aspects of a person also "monitor" the temperament of a child, it will be clear that this "monitoring" is different for children than for adults because the essential aspects of the person have, on the one hand, "not yet been born," and are, on the other hand, not yet fully mature. There is an immense difference whether the Self is wholly and clearly the force behind the person as a whole, or whether that force acts in a veiled form. It is a part of human development which only brushes aside the veils after many years, and the Self creates a content for the temperaments so that they can manifest themselves fully and in an adult way. The following chapter deals in detail with Wolfgang Schad's article and provides a greater insight into the background of the child's temperament.

– 9 –

Up to the age of fourteen

Study of the temperaments forms part of the curriculum for those training to become teachers in Steiner schools. Students do exercises related to the temperaments as described in Rudolf Steiner's *Discussions with Teachers*. Nevertheless, work on the temperaments appears to have only a modest place in the daily curriculum of the training colleges. It is a general experience that the temperament of a child is not very easy to identify and assess, particularly because there are all sorts of combinations which complicate things for us.

In the first of the *Discussions with Teachers* (21 August 1919), Rudolf Steiner discussed the relationship between the essential aspects of a person and the temperaments of children. As we saw above, this relationship is different from that for adults because the essential aspects of a child are still developing. However, the question is how different this relationship is. Rudolf Steiner gives a very precise answer to this: the choleric temperament does not develop from a dominant Self as it does at a later stage, but is located in the astral area. The sanguine temperament is related to the etheric body, which is still very fluid in a child. A child which "lives" entirely in his physical body is a phlegmatic child, and the melancholic tendency is based on the predominance of the Self in the earliest years.

These conclusions immediately give rise to other questions, such as the following: Where does this Self come from when it is not yet there, and how can it later form the basis of the choleric temperament?

In Wolfgang Schad's article mentioned in the previous chapter, this and other questions are raised. The conclusions based on Rudolf Steiner's lectures are not very easy to understand, but anyone interested in the anthroposophical view of the temperaments in children, can consider the explanation as a sort of "working hypothesis." Our insight into these matters is usually insufficient, but we can reflect on these things and this in itself will bring rewards in our practical work.

Schad maintains that the temperament in a child has a mysterious aspect because the essential aspects of a child are different from those of adults. They are actually "coloured" by a different essential aspect, in fact an aspect which is at a higher stage in the ordinary development. The astral body is coloured by the Self, which results in a choleric temperament in a child. However, it is much more closely related to the physical aspect of the child than in an adult.

In a child the etheric body is not yet so stably anchored in the organs as it is in older people, but it is still extremely receptive to all sorts of impressions related to spiritual matters. Any disruption in this area can result in sleeplessness and lack of appetite. When there are quarrels around a child, or, as I once experienced, a mother talks and laughs loudly with visitors, a child may suddenly start to become sick and vomit without any advance warning. When the child is psychologically under pressure he uses his body as an "escape valve."

In anthroposophical terms this is explained by saying that the etheric body is "astrally coloured" and therefore forms the basis of the sanguine temperament of the child. The physical body is also still developing and everything is permeated with etheric forces — this is why a child's physique has such grace. It is the body that forms the basis for the phlegmatic temperament.

The melancholic temperament requires a separate description and will be dealt with later. It seems that this "colour" of our essential aspects is given to us at birth. When we have followed the thought processes which lead to these conclusions, another question arises: where do these innate colours come from? If they are "brought along" does this not take us into the region before birth?

One of Rudolf Steiner's early lecture cycles *(The Theosophy of the Rosicrucians)* describes the special relationship between the essential aspects of a person in one life and the next. If we are prepared to look across the boundaries of life and death and consider Steiner's ideas as provisional concepts, the following quotations about the above-mentioned cycle could provide an answer to these questions:

When a person has used his life well and has had many rich experiences, this means that in the next life the astral body will be born with special gifts in this field. Therefore the experiences and events leave their mark on the astral body of the following incarnation.

However, anything that is perceived, felt, experienced of both pleasure and sorrow, that which is the inner life of the soul, is carried on in the following life in the etheric body and creates certain tendencies there.

Those things which are carried by the etheric body in this life — the permanent character, the talents and disposition — return in the next life in the physical body. For example, a person who has developed bad tendencies and passions in one life can be born with an unhealthy body in the the next life.

Thus we live from the inside out: any aspects of joy, suffering, sorrow and pain in the astral body reappear in the etheric body; any drives and passions rooted in the etheric body reappear as the constitution of the physical body. Our deeds on earth, however, for which we need the physical body, reappear as outward circumstances influencing us in a following incarnation.

In other words, it is not only in our destiny that we come up against ourselves, but also in the tendencies, drives, imagination, predispositions, character and nature which we encounter in ourselves. It is as though every aspect of a person goes through a sieve and reappears in a more refined state in a "lower" aspect of the person.

On the basis of this life here and now, we shall therefore conclude that the astral body is influenced by the "sediment" of the Self in a previous life. In the same way, the present etheric body is also formed by the "sediment" of the previous astral body, and the physical body acquired its constitution from what an earlier etheric body had in the way of inclinations and habits.

Looking back on Rudolf Steiner's words on temperaments in this light, we find to our surprise, when we take a very careful look, that the sheen of a previous life can be observed in a child's early years. These gifts from a previous life, both positive and negative aspects, are transformed in the years needed for this, as described above.

The most mysterious temperament of all four is the melancholic temperament, which is related in children to the Self. In an adult it is caused by the dominance of the physical body. This aspect of the person does not pass through the "sieve." The footsteps we leave on earth remain in the earth. We are born with the tendency to rediscover these old footsteps and situations in individuals to whom we were connected.

This is what is known as our "destiny." In our youth it has not yet entered the body, but is all around us. The child is still one with the surrounding world and only gradually distances himself and separates himself from the surrounding world to acquire a sense of his own physical being. Initially, the Self lives outside where it encounters the consequences of a previous physical life. In this case, the Self provides the "character of the environment."

Sometimes an aspect of this remains in the memory — traces in our body, scars revealing injuries which must have caused pain, though this pain is linked to the sharp stones on the mountain path on which the child stumbled and grazed his shins, or the pointed piece of bamboo in the forbidden structure which he climbed despite warnings not to, the sharp point which pierced his arm when he slipped and which he never mentioned because he was too embarrassed ...

Looking into the eyes of a newborn child we see the profound seriousness, the reflection of a distant past. A personality is looking at us, with knowledge and wisdom. When this remains dominant for a long time, it results in a melancholic temperament in a child.

– 10 –

After twice seven years

Looking at photographs of our childhood we sometimes get the feeling "that's not me," and this is certainly true — it is no longer us. We change completely every seven years, not only as regards our outer "coat," but also our feelings, perceptions, wishes, needs and the way in which we see the world. All these change. It is as though we burst out of our old skin, again and again, when the new skin has fully developed. Only our Self is permanent and our own. However, as we get older we find that it is no longer so easy to say: "That's not me." After the age of forty we have to recognize that this is the body which we have to make do with in this life, and we constantly feel connected to it. The same applies to our temperament. At first it is not really our own temperament yet. The background is still moving and all sorts of things have come with us which have to be transformed into the building blocks of this life. However, there comes a stage in development when the own temperament begins to crystallize.

In his collection of lectures, *The Four Temperaments,* Rudolf Steiner describes the difference between the temperaments of children and adults in a drawing which is reproduced below.

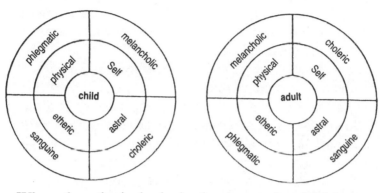

When the etheric body is dominant, the child has a sanguine temperament, while the adult has a phleg-matic temperament. When the Self is dominant, the child is melancholic, while the adult is choleric. When the physical aspect is dominant, the child becomes phlegmatic, but in the adult the relationship to the physical body has changed and this is reflected in the temperament: in this case, the adult tends towards the melancholic. When the astral aspect is dominant, the child tends to be choleric, but when the astral body is separated after the age of fourteen, is "born" and openly has an influence, the growing person in-creasingly has the qualities of a sanguine temper-ament. Thus the complicated subject of the changing relationship between the essential aspects of a person and the temperament are represented in a simple dia-gram. When the outer ring of the child's circle is turned through ninety degrees, we see the whole pattern of the temperaments changing into the adult situation.

This change of the temperaments obviously does not take place from one day to the next. We saw how a person needs four times seven years to become a mature and balanced person with a Self. However, the most dramatic change takes place around the age of fourteen. The shift in the temperaments is part of this whole "internal restructuring" during puberty and the following years of adolescence. As a result of the birth of the astral body, all sorts of — often very striking — changes take place. A girl may suddenly be troubled by allergies which have never been a problem before. A boy may notice that his hair starts to become curly, while up to that time it was completely straight without even a hint of a wave. At the same time that these external characteristics appear, there are shifts in the temperaments, or perhaps it would be more correct to say that this shift causes the external changes.

During her time at primary school, one of our daughters certainly belonged to the choleric type. Her teacher confirmed this. However, as she became older, her face changed dramatically. To her great delight, her short, straight hair started to grow and even started to wave a bit. After about a year, I noticed that her whole manner had become sanguine: she was untidy, full of whims, outgoing and happy. The undercurrent of melancholy was responsible for maintaining a balance.

In this child I was able to observe the change from one temperament to another quite clearly. From this experience I must conclude that it is much easier to see this in some children than in others. These extremely complex years of adolescence may be very tempestuous in one child, while they may pass almost unnoticed in another, but anyone who enjoys following the development in young people as they grow up can learn to see these fascinating changes.

In conclusion, we would like to say that children wear their temperament like a borrowed coat. They have to grow into it, because their own personality has not yet been born. This "coat" is modified and altered until it fits. In an adult a temperament is a window through which the Self manifests itself. The dominant essential aspect continues to dominate throughout a person's life, but there is a shift in their temperament and this is filled with the Self only after many years.

With regard to children, it is the teacher's task to break through the one-sided aspect of the temperament by means of a variety of educational and didactic measures. As adults, we have the responsibility to work on the possibilities of the other temperaments which we also have in ourselves, and to develop them in order to protect the "dominant" aspect from one-sidedness.

The ancient builders of cathedrals knew the secret of the co-operation between the four elements. By mixing earth, air, fire and water, they achieved the warm glow which is present in cathedrals when the sun shines through the stained glass windows. It is a multicoloured glow in which we can fully experience our humanity.

——— o Θ o ———

A memory

She must have been fifteen when she came across that terrible photo. She knew about it, the prize photo by the edge of the swimming pool after a race she had won in the burning tropical sun, but this was the first time she had really seen it. She suddenly saw the way she was standing there, curved like a letter "S." Awful! Did she really walk like that and did she still walk like that years later? If so, it had to stop. She pulled her shoulders back so that her back and neck stretched. She pulled in her stomach muscles and forced herself to walk tall. This required courage, because it meant she had to look straight at the world and she was rather afraid of this. This was why she often walked with her head bent forward, "looking for coins." In future she would walk straight, look people in the eye, take the initiative, confront problems and do all the things she had avoided up to that time. After practising for months, this new attitude became part of her. She had grown into it and she knew she would never look like that old photograph again. All the same, she kept it as a reminder, as a warning and in gratitude.

– 11 –

The number of the earth

According to the insights of spiritual science, the four aspects of man form the basis of the four temperaments. Now that we are familiar with the principle and have seen it in diagrammatic form, it is time to move on. This can lead us along various paths. For example, it is exciting to speculate what the number four actually means qualitatively. Why should there be four essential aspects of a person and four temperaments? Where and when did this number four appear and what can it tell us? First of all, we shall see how the number four has a place in our lives and in our culture. Chapter 14 will deal with fairy tales in which the numbers three and four alternate and supplement each other. Finally, we will try to understand the essence of this angular square; on the one hand, on the basis of ancient writings, and on the other hand, in relation to modern art.

The number four is not only a sign of quantity; traditionally it has also been associated with quality. Four is the number of the earth, as we can discover in a wide variety of aspects: four elements, four seasons, four points of the compass. Starting closer to home, a healthy pregnancy lasts forty weeks. This is followed by the birth of the physical body and the incarnation of a previously invisible individual has started. As we know, the process is not yet complete and will continue. But this is our starting point on earth.

In some areas where there are still many old customs surrounding birth and death, the nursing mother is told strictly to rest for forty days. After this period, ordinary life starts again. The newborn child gives the first sign of true contact after this period of forty days because it begins to smile when it sees its mother.

Exodus, the second book of the Old Testament, describes the Israelites departing from Egypt to find their own land. They had to walk through the desert for forty years before they had formed a close community, based on strict laws and years of hardship, hunger and thirst. When they found the promised land they became a nation.

In the past, when animals or plants were imported into a country they had to be quarantined for forty days to see whether they contained any germs which might be dangerous to the indigenous flora or fauna. This period of forty days, or weeks or years, seems to be necessary to "prove" whether something is viable. Before that time things are not so certain. When Noah went into the Ark with his family and all his animals, the rain stopped after forty days and the water began to recede. In Noah, humanity had a chance to start again.

The Greek philosopher Heraclitus said that everything was created from fire. Reading through the Genesis story of the Creation in the Old Testament, we find that the element of heat was already present, as

well as the air and water. The element of the earth did
not yet exist. Order was created from chaos and form
was created with the creation of the element of the
earth. The process of Creation lasted six days, starting
with the first words: *Let there be light!* Light makes
things clear; what was diffuse and unified became
divided, the various elements were separated, and each
found its own place. This process culminated in the
creation of man, who stood and walked on earth,
leaving his footsteps on it. This was the beginning of
incarnation and the fourth element was born.

An old book of hours dating from the eleventh
century, safely stored away in the Munich City Library,
contains a wonderful miniature. It is an unorthodox
representation of the descent of the Holy Ghost at
Pentecost. A clover leaf has been drawn in a square; it
does not have three leaves like an ordinary clover leaf,
but is the rare four-leafed clover. Three disciples are
depicted in a curve of each leaf. In the middle there is
a dove, the sign of the Holy Ghost, radiating twelve
rays. Each ray ends in three points. They look like the
sun hands in the Egyptian Akhnaton period. They are
also reminiscent of the rays of compass-cards, like the
one found in the paving stones of the square in front of
St Peter's Basilica in Rome. The Gospel according to
St John says: "The wind blows wherever it pleases,"
referring to the Holy Ghost. The four times three
disciples represent the whole of developing humanity.

This complicated subdivision into four times three
can also be found in our western calendar, the division
of the year into four seasons, each comprising three

months. This is what remains of the ancient Babylonian astrology which ordered time on earth in a meaningful way in accordance with cosmic laws.

The fact that these laws also have an effect on our body was known many centuries ago, as is shown, for example, in the many illustrations of so-called "astrological man." There is a beautiful example of this in the *Book of Hours of the Duc de Berry (c.*1400). A sign of the zodiac is incorporated with each illustration of the four important "regions" of the human figure. We carry the year in our body, from our head to our feet. The idea that a particular star sign is related to a particular part of our body was part of the system on which medical science was based in those times.

There are other examples of iconology which express the quality of the number four. Just as the twelve disciples represent the whole of humanity and all the possible variations are in this way meaningfully summarized, the four Evangelists have traditionally been seen as four types of man who each described the Gospel of Jesus Christ from their own distinctive viewpoint. As individuals they were given their own sign, a symbol which emphasized their individual character. However, as they were often depicted together in a group, it is clear that they were experienced as an organic whole in which the four parts worked together and supplement each other.

In the tympanum of the royal portal of the Cathedral of Notre Dame in Chartres, there is a relief known as the *Majestas Domini.* Christ is enthroned in an oval surround, accompanied by the four apocalyptic beasts which symbolize the four Evangelists: Matthew as a winged human figure, Mark as a winged lion, Luke as a winged bull, and John as an eagle. The incarnation of the Word is described in four ways, each one-sided in itself, but together leading us to the *quinta essentia* mentioned by Paracelsus. He meant something different, but the image is the same. The outer figures leave their vantage points, and the movement towards each other creates something new in the centre which transcends their one-sidedness: a new balance, a new truth.

In the following chapter, I will describe how the four Evangelists can enrich the background for our ideas on the temperaments.

– 12 –

The four Evangelists

It was very quiet in the house; the youngest children still had a nap in the afternoons. In the play area in front of the low sofa, a little girl was piling one wooden brick on another with great concentration. Methodically she started using all the plain bricks in the basket to build a fantastic structure consisting of a tower with a broad base, becoming narrower as it rose up, with a logical construction and balanced shape. Then she built other towers which were thinner, more like pillars, this time also using the coloured bricks. Every time she placed one brick on another the little girl checked the balance so that the tower would not fall over. One of the towers was made up of cylindrical bricks — there must have been ten of them — with a sort of yellow bridge on its side on the top, a smaller cube on top of that, finally crowned with a broad, thick, long piece of wood. It was placed flat on the extremely thin pillar, but was balanced so meticulously that the tower remained standing until all the blocks had been used and all the cuddly toys, dolls and other animals had been grouped around the main structure, and all the cars, gates and other vehicles had formed a wall around this unusual city.

Every child builds, but children do not all build in the same way. One child will work systematically to create real structures enclosing spaces which can be inhabited. Another child will place the bricks arbitrarily next to each other, apparently without any structure and open on all sides, so that the building never looks finished. A third child will not make towers or houses, but always bridges. They all build in their own way, but they all build, because this is how their own young bodies are built up through the years by an invisible builder. When we bring them up we can contribute to this process.

Some people continue to build throughout their lives. St Matthew must have been one of these people. The first of the four Gospels comes down to us demonstrating a fixed order in things: it starts by summarizing three times fourteen generations. In the same way as a bricklayer picks up his bricks and taps them with a trowel to check that they are in the correct position, Matthew piles one name on top of the other to form a powerful structure and concludes: "So all the generations from Abraham to David were fourteen generations, and from David to the deportation to Babylon fourteen generations, and from the deportation to Babylon to the Christ fourteen generations" (Matt.1). In Chapter 5 he builds another one of these close-knit structures; the Sermon on the Mount, in which the bricks are the striking repetitions which introduce the many warnings, commandments and prohibitions: "Blessed are the poor in spirit ... blessed are those who hunger and thirst for righteousness ... blessed are the peacemakers ..." and further on: "You have heard that it was said to the men of old ...," followed by one of the Ten Commandments which is given a different, Christian interpretation. Just after Palm Sunday this is repeated again in a final "thundering sermon" to the Pharisees: "Woe to you, scribes and Pharisees!" (23:13)

The formative force of the laws and commandments are the most striking elements of this Gospel. They are never quoted and mentioned as often anywhere else. There is a strong link with the past which is revealed in the summary of the many generations at the beginning. Matthew links the Old Testament with the New Testament by being the first of the four Evangelists. This is also revealed in the tightly knit composition of this Gospel: the first chapter evokes the name "Emmanuel" which means "God with us," and ends with the words of the risen Christ: "And lo, I am with you always, to the close of the age." (28:20) This ancient formula acquires a new shining meaning which can inspire us today and in the future.

The Gospel according to Mark provides us with a completely different image. While Matthew builds up his description of the life of Jesus Christ in broad and thorough terms with the emphasis on the doctrine, the commandments, the laws and many parables, the second Evangelist describes this in a very short and powerful way. St Mark was a man of few words and his Gospel is the shortest of all four. While Matthew needed a long introduction and introduced John the Baptist only in Chapter 3, Mark goes straight in at the deep end.

He does not begin with the birth of a child, but starts straightaway in Chapter 1 with the baptism in the Jordan. From a spiritual point of view this was also a birth, that of the figure of Christ in the adult man Jesus. Immediately after the baptism in the Jordan, Mark describes how the first disciples were called and there is a dramatic encounter with an "evil spirit." This is followed by the healing of a leper, and a woman who is cured of a burning fever. The Gospel is action-packed and moves at a great pace with no long sermons and little reflection. Events follow each other very quickly because deeds and man's actions are important to Mark. It is as though the artist is creating figures from lumps of clay with hurried but assured movements. They are moving figures, moments from the life of Jesus Christ and the people who were affected by his actions and words. St Mark saw his Master as a man who interreacted with other men.

Mark's Gospel is often read at Easter because he makes a link between the rising sun and the Resurrection in his account of the event: "Early on the first day of the week, they went to the tomb when the sun had risen." (Mark 16:2) The strength and heat of the sun which awakens plants from their winter sleep is reflected in the words with which St Mark sends the disciples into the world: "Go into all the world and preach the good news to all creation!" The last sentence of this Gospel is characteristic: "And they went forth and preached everywhere, while the Lord worked with them and confirmed the message by the signs that attended it." (16:20) St Mark showed us Christ in action.

The third description of Christ's life is that contained
in the Luke's Gospel. Like Matthew's Gospel, this
contains a register of the generations, though it does
not appear until Chapter 3. Furthermore, the names are
given in reverse order. While Matthew starts the
register with the first patriarch, Abraham, and concludes with the name of Jesus Christ, the series in
Luke's Gospel starts with Jesus "who was about thirty
years of age," and ends with "the son of Seth, the son
of Adam, the son of God." This sequence of names
goes back not to an earthly father, but to a heavenly
Father. The Christian prayer, "Our Father," which is
found only in Luke's Gospel in this form also contains
the words: "Hallowed be thy name." Luke's Gospel
does start with the birth, and even with a double birth:
that of John, whose father was the ancient priest
Zachariah, and that of the child Jesus, with the young
mother Mary. It also describes the shepherds in the
fields who hear the angels sing and receive a message.
The whole story is permeated with an atmosphere
which is not of this world. There is a haze of joyful
peace hanging over this Gospel which is rather like we
imagine paradise where a young, newly created being
looks around in astonishment at all the beauty around
him. He is all eyes and all ears, smells the flowers,
strokes the animals, tastes the fruit. The young person
is made up completely of the senses and is open to the
world as innocent as a child, enjoying everything that
Mother Earth has to offer. There is no awareness of
past or future, just the constant creation of the present
which is familiar to us from very young children. The

delightful mobility of a child has a quality which we can keep in ourselves as a gift from God until a great age. This inner mobility also allows us to make mistakes, seek adventure and try out new things.

Only St Luke relates the parable of the Prodigal Son: "There was a man who had two sons." The older stayed at home while the younger went into the wide world to learn from his adventures what his father's house meant to him. He returned in dire poverty and utter misery, making it possible for him to be "found." It is easier for man to "pass through the eye of a needle" and remain open to the world of the angels if he is unburdened by wealth, whether this consists of earthly goods, busy activities or spiritual gifts (compare Luke 10, 16 and 18). Up to the very last lines of this Gospel there is a possibility of "repentance and forgiveness of sins." This refers to the mobility of the soul.

The Gospel according to St John, the last Gospel written by the apostle "who experienced the love of Jesus," is the most elevated and most spiritual of all four Gospels, and starts with the grandiose lines:

> In the beginning was the Word, and the Word was with God, and the Word was God. He was in the beginning with God. All things were made through him, and without him was not anything made that was made.

This means that everything that was created came from the spirit. Anyone who views and sees all earthly things and all matter including his own body in this way, must be an initiate who can hear "the music of the spheres," as it was known in past centuries. Like no other, St John was familiar with the physical body containing a force which reveals the divine aspect. From St John's Gospel we learn to see that the physical body is an expression or crystallization of the spirit. It is not necessary to go back to the Middle Ages to see the astonishing and special laws operating in the body. The body is created in such a way that it can bear the spirit. The physical substance, which literally means "that which stands underneath," forms the foundation for a higher spiritual substance. In his Gospel, St John links earthly reality with cosmic and spiritual levels and does so by means of the Word, for which Man is a sounding board. The seven "I am" words, resonate like the seven bugles from the Book of the Apocalypse by the same author. "I am the true vine ... I am the bread of life ... I am the way, the truth and the life." Another theme which recurs in this account in different keys is the Resurrection: one form of being is resurrected from another. In the nighttime discussion with Nicodemus (Ch.3) there is a reference to "rebirth," and to the need to be reborn from above. To the Greeks, he said: "Unless a grain of wheat falls into the earth and dies, it remains alone. But if it dies, it bears much fruit." (12:24). The sickness, death and raising of Lazarus is described in great detail (Ch.11).

The Trinity is another theme in John; the whole Gospel is full of the "three-in-one" of the Father, the Son and the Holy Ghost. At the end these two themes are interwoven in the powerful dialogue between the

Risen Son and the Disciple Peter. "Simon, Son of John, do you love me more than they?" This is repeated three times to restore the balance which has been broken by the three denials.

The fourth theme is also contained in this last dialogue — the theme of love: "This is my commandment, that you love one another as I have loved you," as he tells the disciples in his last conversation before his death (15:12). For St John this was the factor which connected all things: heaven and earth, body and spirit.

——— o Θ o ———

There is a painting by Rembrandt which shows St Matthew as a wise old man with a whitish grey beard. The man does not look at us, but looks into the distance. With great concentration he listens to the words whispered into his ear by an angel. His hand, holding a goose quill, rests on the book in front of him, and his other hand is placed on his heart, dividing his beard, in the way in which Moses is often depicted. This was Rembrandt's view of the builder of words, faithful to tradition, and connecting the old with the new in a precise, meticulous way. Do we recognize the phlegmatic element in ourselves? When we are old enough we will know it in the years known as the twilight years. It brings the wisdom of old age.

Dürer painted a striking portrait of Mark as a powerful man with a full curly beard, dark hair, a powerful bull neck and sparkling dark brown eyes. In other words, as a young man full of strength. It is the image of a conqueror, of a man of action who knows what he wants. We carry this aspect in ourselves when we are young and go out into the world full of promise. The second stage of life, up to the age of twenty-eight, is characterized by a fiery enthusiasm and wild hair. The choleric aspect is predominant during this period.

The name of Luke may have some echoes of the Latin word "lux," meaning light. There is no doubt that this Gospel shines as a light in the world and has brought true joy to mankind through the centuries. St Luke was a doctor and the companion of the apostle Paul, whose letters tell us about him. Luke was fascinated by Christ's healing powers. For him, this was the expression of the infinite stream of love radiated by the Son of God. There is a medieval legend that Luke painted a picture of the Virgin Mary. For example, Roger van der Weyden depicted him in this way. There is also a seventeenth century engraving by Jacques Callot, a vignette in a book of saints, which shows Luke as a young man sitting at an easel. He is looking up at a cloud where Mary poses for him with the child. Another painting in the church of Santa Maria Maggiore in Rome is said to be the work of Luke.

Whatever the truth of the matter, anyone who reads the Gospel according to St Luke will come across the image of the Madonna again and again. It is so beautiful that even the English playwright, George Bernard Shaw, who was feared for his sharp tongue, allegedly once said that the Saviour conquered the hearts of men through the Madonna in Luke's Gospel. This is the natural way in which a child does so. It is the heart-warming joy of the sanguine temperament which gives the first stage of life a warm glow and to which we think back nostalgically in the course of our lives.

"He who has an ear, let him hear what the Spirit says to the churches." These are the words said repeatedly in the letters to the seven churches in the Revelation to St John. The National Library in Paris contains a perfectly preserved illustrated Apocalypse, dated c.1400. Each page shows St John surrounded by scenes from the Apocalypse. On page 4, he is sitting on the ground with a narrow strip of white paper on his knee. His pen almost pricks through the parchment as he writes. The white dove of the Holy Spirit flies over his head: "And to the angel of the church in Sardis write: ... you have the name of being alive, and you are dead." (3:1). His head is filled with the Spirit, and at his feet there is a rattling skeleton. There is no more conceivable characteristic representation of St John.

When we pass the age of forty we become aware that the strength of youth is declining. We have become fully incarnate and enter the melancholic stage of our lives. However, we are given another fourteen years to discover the spiritual side of our bodily frame. This is the double nature of the melancholy aspect, the two sides which traditionally go with St John: mind and matter, eagle and scorpion, the highest and the lowest.

Each Evangelist has his own symbol, a symbol which reveals an essential aspect of his being. These are described in the Book of Revelation:

> And round the throne, on each side of the
> throne, are four living creatures, full of eyes
> in front and behind. The first living creature
> like a lion, the second living creature like an
> ox, the third living creature with the face of a
> man, and the fourth living creature like a
> flying eagle. And the four living creatures,
> each of them with six wings, are full of eyes
> all round and within, and day and night they
> never cease to sing: "Holy, holy, holy is the
> Lord God Almighty, who was, and is, and is
> to come." (4:6-8).

There are four Evangelists, four types of people, four possible ways in which the human soul can manifest itself. In the lecture course for teachers which Rudolf Steiner gave in 1923, I came across a strange remark. In his introduction Steiner says that teachers must ensure that the religious element in education is taken into account and put into practice in their work. It is not necessary to refer to God all the time; it is more a matter of a basic religious approach.

This is followed by some rather curious advice for us modern people: The western European Christian tradition should be used to move the spiritual forces deep within us, by constantly "feeding" us with the heart-warming mood of the Gospel according to St Luke. Then he goes on to say that those who want to awaken the deepest ideals in their pupils would do well to look carefully at St John's Gospel. However, in order to ensure that "their" children are well grounded in their lives and do not avoid problems, teachers should carefully read St Mark's Gospel. Finally, if it is important to them that children grow up to become people who do not pass things by, but take careful note of things, teachers should be inspired by the Gospel according to St Matthew.

Of this advice to teachers, Steiner goes on to say: "However, this can also be said in a different way which is no less religious or Christian." He adds that it is also possible to study the four temperaments of man and to learn to distinguish and learn to deal with them. What are the characteristics of a choleric person? How do you deal with a melancholic person? What do you do with a sanguine pupil, and where do you put a group of phlegmatic pupils?

> In fact, what I said about the four Gospels is basically exactly the same, at least as regards the spirit, because it leads to the same elements of the life of man. It is not possible to understand how the Gospels can serve as a strong stimulus for the human soul if, on the other hand, one is not able to translate this into the way in which the temperaments leave their mark on a person as long as he remains on earth.

If we take this advice to heart, we can help our children to grow up to become balanced builders of the future.

– 13 –

The black square

When the painter, Kazimir Malevich, died in Leningrad in May 1935 he was taken to his burial in a manner which suited his style. The coffin was transported on a small lorry. A print of what was to become the most famous painting of the *avant garde* was attached between the headlights of the lorry. It was a black square on a white background, the most radical expression: of a design which aimed at total abstraction. Although Malevich had returned in his later work to a figurative style of painting, his funeral procession showed that for people around him his life had been expressed by that black square. His attempt to achieve forms created purely with colour and line — the fundamentals of art — had led him to this minimalist expression, after he had started to reject recognizable forms derived from the natural world. Through taking this direction, the creator of forms can achieve an abstract expression, that is, an extract, a concentrated substance of visible reality from which the artist must "see" the idea contained within and express it with his own skill. The artist reads the painting as he or she would read a book. After all, letter characters are also an abstraction, a collection of signs from which the ideas, the spiritual substance contained in them, must be awakened by reading.

Black is the absolute zero, death without hope, the physical body which disintegrates without life. However, in Malevich, black has acquired a form, an outline which contrasts strikingly with the white of the background. This white is not reminiscent of life, but rather of the icy crystal floor of the Snow Queen in Hans Christian Andersen's tale.

The square has always been the sign for earthly elements in occult writings. The earth itself was viewed as being round and flat, as revealed in a Bible illustration dating from the thirteenth century. The Creator supports the earth, round as a wheel, in his left hand, while with his right hand, he places the point of an enormous pair of compasses in the centre of the circle with the circumscribing arm on the circumference. The earth is the yellow lump of clay in the centre of the wheel; around this there is the firmament with the sun, the moon and the stars, followed by a line of clouds like vegetation and a wavy line of water. The four elements concisely contained.

Another manuscript shows the earthly element as a square in which the corners are filled with circles. These circles contain four elements; again the sky looks like a peculiar form of vegetation, with cauliflower clouds. In the centre, Christ is represented as a young man with the earth like a ball under his feet.

The square shape can also be seen in the early Christian baptistries. There are good examples of this in Ravenna, such as the baptistry commissioned by the Aryan King of the Goths, Theoderic (fifth century) and the beautiful baptistry of the Duomo in Florence with its famous bronze doors. These baptistries were built in the shape of an octagon which contains two squares, one placed at an angle to the other.

When man is born, he enters the world of the elements. The spiritual qualities of the four elements, which Goethe would call archetypes, live in the spiritual world which he has left behind. The child is baptized in the centre of these two overlapping squares so that this sacred event is not only expressed in the words of the sacrament of Baptism, but the shape of the space also reveals that man is a citizen of two worlds. In the "true and miraculous story of Mariken van Nieumeghen, who lived and communed with the devil for more than seven years" (c.1500), Moenen, the Devil, promises that he will teach the girl whom he has tempted the seven liberal arts condition that she changes her name, Mariken, because this name reminds him of "a certain Maria" of whom he does not wish to be reminded. "Call yourself Lijnken, Grietken or Lijsken."

The girl does not realize what she is dealing with and is surprised that anyone should be offended by "the noblest and sweetest name in the world." She accepts that she may not cross herself in his presence, but insists on retaining her name.

Then the Devil comes up with a solution: "I will be satisfied if you keep the first letter of your name, virtuous lady. That is the 'M,' so you will be called Emmeken."

Then the girl is initiated into a variety of secret and public arts so that she can acquire wealth as a free person, and no longer needs God. On their travels through the country, Moenen recommends her to farmers and citizens: "She wants to perform even more miracles. You won't see her equal in your lifetime. She's expert in all the seven liberal arts: astronomy and geometry, arithmetic, logic and grammar, music and rhetoric."

These "seven liberal arts" are represented on the west gate of the Cathedral in Chartres as seven noblewomen. In the Middle Ages they constituted the foundation of study at every respectable university. They made up the universal basic training which students followed to become educated. They could then choose a specific subject to earn their living. These seven liberal arts were divided into two groups, the *trivium* and the *quadrivium,* as shown in the diagram below:

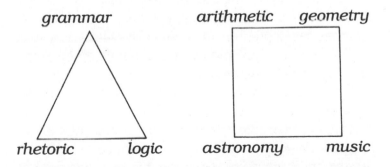

In the figure on the left *(trivium)*, language is central. In the figure on the right *(quadrivium)*, the elements of measure, weight and number are the central theme. All of science has developed from this, and all the science subjects. The young girl, Emmeken, was initiated into the secrets and laws of the word, but in natural science, only tangible and measurable aspects applied, at least officially. The fact that the other side of reality cannot be denied, and that the transposed square of the invisible world increasingly reveals its reality is apparent from all sorts of phenomena in our time.

We encounter the square elsewhere in the new form of the sacrament of Baptism as it takes place in The Christian Community, the movement for religious renewal. Apart from water as a life-giving force, there is salt. Salt contains a strong formative force. When there is too much salt, the flow of life is inhibited and growth is not possible. When there is too much salt in the soil, there can be no life — after the disastrous floods of 1953 in Holland, it was several years before the salt-impregnated soil of Zeeland was rinsed clean and could bear fruit again. The basic shape of the salt crystal is a square, and this is the sign with which the substance is applied to the chin of a child when it is christened. The chin, and in fact the whole of the lower jaw, is the most mobile part of the head, and is connected with the will. By performing the sign of the square in this place, the act expresses a prayer that formative forces may have an effect on the child's will — the area which withdraws most from consciousness. As the child grows up, he draws his own body like a house where he wishes to live, and the basic shape of this house is a square. There are windows and a door, and the house is often lit up from inside. Sometimes the person who lives there is shown next to the house, but one day he will suddenly be inside the house, standing in front of the window. Much later, the child starts to draw everything that is inside the square house. It is as though he is saying: "I have taken possession of the house. I have moved in. It has become my house." This is the time at which the child is ready to go to school and the first permanent teeth replace the milk teeth which are lost. This is the time related to the formative force of salt. The qualities of water, which contains more movement, are more appropriate for the very young child. By the time the child goes to school, demands are imposed, and he must learn to understand his limits in many areas. The period from the age of seven to fourteen is the ideal time for the development of the memory. At Steiner schools, multiplication tables are literally stamped with the feet and clapped with the hands.

———— o Θ o ————

There is another place where Malevich's black square has an interesting equivalent. In Mecca there is a large black cube, the Ka'aba, the holy shrine of Islam. In the world of spirit, however, its counterpart exists in the new city described "in all its radiance and glory," in the vision which St John had on the island of Patmos. Because of his Jewish background, the Apostle called this celestial city the "new Jerusalem."

"Its radiance like a most rare jewel, like a jasper, clear as crystal." The city has twelve gates and is based on twelve foundations decorated with gems. St John continues:

> And he who talked to me had a measuring rod of gold to measure the city and its gates and walls. The city lies foursquare, its length the same as its breadth: and he measured the city with his rod, twelve thousand stadia; its length and breadth and height are equal. He also measured its wall, a hundred and forty-four cubits, by a man's measure, that is, an angel's. (21:15-17).

The new Jerusalem is a city which is based on a square, but in three dimensions it is a cube with six square faces, six aspects between which we find ourselves: in front and behind, left and right, top and bottom. In other words, we orient ourselves according to the past and future in order to understand the present. We either act or wait, listening. We stand on earth and look up at the sky. I believe that this third dimension gives a meaning to our existence, so that the black square can become dear to us, and we can perform the task which is contained in a Persian proverb: "Love the earth so that it will become a shining gem."

– 14 –

Fairy tales as a guide

Anyone familiar with fairy tales knows how often the number three recurs in them. In the story of *Rumpelstiltskin,* the miller's daughter has to spin straw into gold three times before she can marry the king. Later, to avoid having to surrender her first child as the price for the goblin's help, she is allowed three guesses to discover the goblin's name.

In fairy tales where the hero or heroine travels through the world in disguise, performing the meanest tasks, there is often a moment when they must show themselves in their true guise three times. The changed aspect of their clothes reveals that this has taken place: Thousandfurs appears the first time in a garment "as golden as the sun," then in a cloak "as silver as the moon," and the third time in a garment "as radiant as the stars." In the story of *Cinderella,* the girl goes to the ball on three successive nights, wearing gowns of increasing splendour. In the fairy tale, *Iron Hans,* the disguised son of the king appears at the tournament as an unknown knight, first wearing red armour, then white, and finally clad entirely in black.

The recurrence of the number three in these fairy

tales reflects a process related to what is meant in the saying, "Third time lucky." Such tales and sayings give us a glimpse into the great foundation of our human existence which in the Christian tradition is called the *Sancta Trinitas,* or principle of Three-in-One. However, this trinity is embedded in a fourth element, which renders these processes visible, the earthly element. In the stories, this fourth element is represented by the figure of the girl or young man who "physically" experiences the process.

However, we also encounter the number four in fairy tales where it has a particular quality. Let us take a closer look at three stories. Some of the fairy tales from the Germanic language area, such as those collected by the Brothers Grimm, are almost too well known. However, there are others which are less known and these often prove to contain treasures which can pass us by unless someone points them out to us. Rudolf Geiger's masterful analysis of the strange tale, *The Four Clever Brothers,* is a good example.

As so often in the Grimm tales, the figures in the story often form a whole person. All four brothers we are told about are represented in us. The strange brothers live together in their father's house. They are poor, and as is the case in dire poverty, something has to happen. The brothers go out into the wide world to learn a trade. At a crossroads each brother goes his own way. The oldest becomes a skilled thief. The second becomes an accomplished astronomer. The third becomes a hunter who never misses his quarry, and the fourth becomes an extremely deft tailor. They have

four years in which to perfect their trade. At the end of
their apprenticeship they return to their father where
they have to perform a test to show what they can do.
The surprising thing is that they can only pass the test
by working together. When they have successfully
completed it, their father says: "There will be a time
when you will need your art. Just wait!"

When the time comes it becomes clear that again
they can only succeed by working together, and so they
succeed in rescuing the king's daughter from the
dragon's lair. For their reward, the four brothers are
each given half a kingdom, which means that they can
rule over the kingdom, two by two.

In the four trades of the skilled brothers, Geiger
shows that we can discover the four essential aspects
of man. The two divided kingdoms are heaven and
earth, the two areas where man is "at home." They are
as different as day and night. The thief and the astronomer need the night for their work, like the Self and the
astral body. The hunter and the tailor use the light of
day to work on earth, just as man's etheric and physical body belong to the day and the earth.

Another Grimm's tale also reveals these four essential aspects playing a role, not in as perfect a way as in
the previous story, which describes a future ideal, but
more as they work here and now, in people and above
all between people. The story is *The Two Travelling
Companions*. The light and the dark guides of life meet
each other: the cobbler who knows his customers from
the shoes with which they leave their footprints in the
earth, and the tailor whose greatest joy is to make

beautiful clothes for other people. He is a happy, friendly man and therefore attracts a lot of customers. But he generously shares the money he earns with his less fortunate companion. He has the compassion to help his friend, and even animals are inclined to help him when he is in need. But he is light-hearted and pays a heavy price for this, losing the sight from his eyes. However, anyone who is blind in this earthly world can see in another world.

Later, as the result of the intervention of the jealous cobbler, he is commissioned by the king to perform four tasks. These four tasks are the relevant aspect of the story. What can the images tell us? For the first task, the tailor has to find a golden crown that was lost in ancient times. A duck with twelve ducklings fishes this crown up from a pond and the friendly tailor receives a golden chain as his reward.

For the second task he has to make a copy of the royal castle out of wax, not leaving out a single nail in the wall. Bees fly into the castle crawling into every nook and cranny to examine it carefully. Then they fly back and build a copy of the castle in fragrant wax. The tailor is rewarded with a house of stone.

Then the evil cobbler thinks of a third task: "The tailor had heard that no water would well up in the castle yard and he dared to say that he would make the water spurt up in the middle of the yard as high as a man and as clear as crystal." This time the tailor is helped by a foal, by this time a full-grown creature. And what did the king do when the task was completed? He embraced the tailor in everyone's presence.

For the fourth task the tailor has to provide something else that is lacking: the king has daughters but no
son. It is a stork which fulfils this last task and it
comes as no surprise to learn that the tailor is then per-
mitted to marry the king's oldest daughter.

What is the relationship between these images and
the four essential aspects of man? The first task con-
cerns a duck. During archaeological excavations in
Italy, Etruscan wedding gifts with a curious motif were
discovered: two ducks with twelve ducklings on a
fibula, a long pin for attaching a loose garment to the
shoulder. The duck with her ducklings is an image
which is familiar to us in Holland, as they swim round
in ditches and canals, the downy ducklings in a perfect
line behind their mother. This image has become a
symbol for the concept of a "generation" or "family."
The number twelve reveals the relationship between the
human figure and its cosmic origin. The tailor's first
task was related to the physical body and its inheritance of many generations.

The second task contains an unusual request — to
copy the royal castle in the most minute detail, in wax,
a living substance which can be easily moulded. Where
did such a crabby cobbler get such a poetic idea? It is
as though the laws on which this task is based are a
result of the four tasks as a whole, that is, of the image
of the fairy tale itself, and not of the logic of the story.
There is something mysterious about a swarm of bees.
It obeys a strong inner discipline as a single unit.
Moreover, bees are the builders of perfect hexagonal
honeycombs.

This image which is taken from earthly reality is at
the same time an image of a higher reality. According
to spiritual science, the bees represent the formative
forces which are produced by the etheric body. The
description of the swarm of bees creating the royal
palace in wax is the most beautiful and loveliest image
of any fairy tale I know.

The third task is achieved with the help of a foal.
The way in which it makes the hidden spring well up
is reminiscent of the winged horse Pegasus, in Greek
mythology. Just as digestion is the characteristic
activity of the cow, the hypersensitive nervous system
is characteristic of the horse. In man the nervous
system is the physical point of contact for the astral
body. The tailor had once out of compassion saved the
foal's life when it was dying of hunger. This resulted
in a moral relationship with the creature and the result
was that living water was able to flow.

This same depth of relationship enabled a stork to
bring a child in the fourth and last task. This was the
germ of new life from the waters of the spirit — the
Self of the son of man.

———— o Θ o ————

There is another very well-known, short fairy tale
which I would like to mention here. It also describes
the four essential aspects of man, but again in an entirely different way. The images are taken from prosaic
everyday reality and it is therefore reminiscent of some

of the parables in the Bible. Anyone who has ears to hear and eyes to see will recognize a higher reality in these everyday images.

There are four animals: a donkey, a dog, a cat and a cockerel, on their way to the city of Bremen. All four have fled from their masters. However, they do not get further than a dark wood, where they decide to spend the night. The cockerel spies a light in the distance when he climbs up in a tree. It turns out to be a house where a band of robbers are enjoying the booty they have stolen. The four animals think of a ruse to get into the house and chase out the robbers. The donkey stands on the windowsill with his front legs, the dog jumps onto the donkey's back, the cat climbs onto the dog and finally the cockerel perches on the cat's head. When they have done this they all start to make music at the same time: the donkey brays, the dog barks, the cat miaows and the cock crows. Then they throw themselves into the room through the window, frightening the terrified robbers away.

The donkey is an archetypal image of the physical body. Working in his "mill of life," the miller sees that his "donkey" is tired and at the end of his tether. St Francis of Assisi called his poor body tormented by disease, "Brother Donkey." The donkey is often obstinate and often goes its own way. This is easy for us to identify with.

The dog is a faithful guard. He takes over his master's habits and follows him like a shadow. He is naturally greedy and we have to keep him under control.

The cat has eyes which can see a mouse move even

in the dark. He likes to be stroked until the sparks fly on his shiny, soft fur. But in general he will go his own way unperturbed. He stalks through the garden, spying on birds. While a dog with its broad chest always has a rather rugged aspect, the cat has a fine and elegant appearance.

Right at the top there is the cockerel. It crows when the dawn breaks, waking people from their sleep. It called to Simon Peter when he strayed off the path and denied his Lord thrice, when he was standing guard:

> And immediately the cock crowed a second time. And Peter remembered how Jesus had said to him: "Before the cock crows twice, you will deny me three times." And he broke down and wept.

Remorse is an activity of the Self.

The language of the fairy tale can enrich us in two ways: on the one hand, it provides us with an image which can bring life to an abstract concept. On the other hand, it can provide surprising perspectives by using ordinary familiar words in such a way that they suddenly acquire depth, an extra dimension, an unsuspected background. The human word regains its full value and becomes as new. We usually use words as a means of communication, but they are much more than this. Words also live in two worlds and words also have a visible and an invisible side. It is this invisible side that is revealed by fairy tales, at least for anyone who has an eye for this.

– 15 –

Moving mountains

In the Caucasus, it is said there is a high mountain where a bird comes to whet its beak once every hundred years. It goes to a rock and sharpens its beak and when the mountain has been worn away one second of eternity has passed.

On average the human spirit has less than a hundred years to whet itself on a human body. The rock does not feel any pain when it is being worn away. As humans, we know the sufferings of both soul and body. Where there is suffering, whether it is apparent or silent, there is a little bird at work. A little piece of the mountain is being worn away and transformed into fertile earth.

The transformation of our temperament requires at least as many bits of eternity. It is an art in itself to describe and discover a temperament: it works in this way and that. It is an even greater art not to stop there but to go on to ask: How can I work on myself in such a way that I am not controlled by my temperament, but that I control it? What are we actually doing when we reflect on someone so as to discover their temperament? We know that person as a whole, as someone with whom we talk, interrelate, discuss, in other words as someone we know in many different situations. There is the field of their experience, and their togetherness with other people. And we ourselves are part of that whole.

However, there is another level in us, the level on which we keep a certain distance from ourselves, from other people and from situations. At this level we can become aware in a wider sense. We can become conscious of another person's response to a situation or to a remark, seeing it in the context of previous responses. Neither the response nor the situation is the same as before but there is room for comparisons. We can become aware, too, that our own responses are part of the overall picture. It may be that our responses and theirs fit well together. But this is not always the case, and we may have the feeling that we are banging ourselves against a brick wall. But it's from the top of the brick wall that we get a better view. As soon as we decide to observe from a different viewpoint, we also start to look at things differently. It is as though we are looking down on the situation with different eyes, from a higher plane from which we can see both parties acting, talking and reacting. Then we start to see certain patterns.

On the basis of our observations we form an inner picture of that other person. We become aware that we take into account their physical being. How does the other person look? Is her head large, or actually quite small in relation to the rest of her? Does she have a long thin neck, or is it actually a broad neck and broad shoulders? Is her back straight or are her shoulders slightly hunched? Are her gestures quick and angular, or tentative or sluggish or cautious? Does her manner of talking or behaving correspond to this in any way?

Two things can happen. When we have formed an image of that other person in this way, we may come to the conclusion that there are some unpleasant aspects and this person should begin changing these. On the other hand, we can also conclude that this happens to be the way she is and we have to accept her as she is and live with it. Neither of these points of view reveals a true commitment, and in any case leaves us, ourselves, still detached and uninvolved.

I believe there is another possibility, though this requires two rare qualities in addition: love and faith. Armed with these, we will find we can resolve a situation without constantly playing the role of victim.

How do we do this? The familiar motto "Practice makes perfect" applies again. We start by looking at ourselves and by modifying our own behaviour and responses. We might like to see the other person reacting differently, but it could be that we can achieve this indirectly, by starting on ourselves. For example, by not getting angry straightaway but counting to ten first and saying something constructive, or by stepping back inwardly and carefully observing what the other person really means.

There are so many different ways of expressing things. What is the other person saying and what is the real hidden meaning of his words? If we are naturally reserved and do not find it easy to go up to someone and ask a question or make a friendly remark, it is worth the trouble to do this anyway, even though it goes against our nature. Initially, it may seem rather insincere because we are not used to it. But the more often we pluck up the courage to get over this, the easier it becomes. In the end it can become "second nature."

In education, educating the Self is a prerequisite. A teacher standing in front of the class has her own temperament, but in her group of thirty or more children, all the temperaments are represented. If she wants to achieve something meaningful for all the children, she will have to learn and acknowledge her own one-sided aspects so that she can compensate for them in her teaching methods. It is true that it is sometimes possible to achieve great things through the one-sidedness of the temperament, and a life without temperaments is simply inconceivable. But on the other hand, this one-sidedness can be destructive if not enough work has been done in the early years.

Rudolf Steiner emphatically warns against the dangers of an "excessive temperament" in children:

> In every temperament there is a small and a great danger of degeneration. When he is young, a choleric person is exposed to the danger that his rage could create in his Self without learning any control. This is the smaller danger. The great danger is the madness with which such a Self pursues a single goal. In a sanguine temperament the small

danger is indecisiveness. The great danger is that the fluctuating feelings can result in insanity. In the phlegmatic temperament the small danger is the lack of interest in the world while the great danger is idiocy and stupidity. In the melancholic temperament the small danger is depression and the possibility that the person will fail to achieve his potential. The great danger is delusions.

In education, it is a matter of monitoring children's temperaments which sometimes visibly cause them to suffer, and steering them into a positive direction. However, the aim is not to blunt them or suppress them. Teachers should not focus pointlessly on what a child does not have, but should concern themselves with what the child does have and work on this, as shown above.

In the next chapter, we discuss how a teacher can achieve this in lessons and at home, although it will be possible to give only broad indications in this short book. Once it becomes clear that working with temperaments can help deepen our insight into people, we will automatically start to develop the practice.

– 16 –

Seeing the wood through the trees

There were two trees in the open field, but they were so close together that their branches had become interlocked into one large tree. The gigantic double crown of leaves towered up like a mountain. In the summer, it was dark green and impenetrable to rain and sun. In the autumn, the flaming colours were outlined against threatening thunderclouds. On a winter's night, it had a breathtaking snow-white beauty when the rain-soaked branches froze and the smallest twigs were wrapped in a layer of transparent ice. The thick dark trunks were clearly visible. They rose up from the snowy plane like pillars bearing this crystal structure. In spring, the tree was radiant against a bright blue sky in its gown of light green foliage.

―――― o Θ o ――――

An average class of young children aged seven to twelve years old, contains all the temperaments and all the combinations, as changeable as all the seasons.

There are many ways of structuring a class to facilitate teaching and controlling it. One of these ways was described by Rudolf Steiner in his *Discussions with Teachers*. The whole class can be divided according to temperaments, so that the quiet groups are in the middle and the restless sanguine and choleric children are on the sides. This has the advantage that the teacher can direct his attention alternately to different groups, for example, when he is telling a story.

Another way of making sure that all the temperaments have their fair share of attention is to see each subject in a way in which the four types are clearly addressed in the material covered in the lessons. For example, in arithmetic the four main types of calculation can be dealt with in relation to the temperaments. Although all children must learn them and practise them, it is possible to vary them in such a way that the teacher can appeal to a particular temperament. For example, adding up is appropriate for phlegmatic children, subtracting for melancholic children, multiplying is related to the sanguine temperament, and choleric children like to divide.

However, for all children it is good to base all arithmetic as far as possible on the calculation as a whole, that is, on the answer, and to show that this result can be arrived at in different ways. In language teaching, there are many possible ways of appealing to different temperaments. In botany, it is possible to describe the four seasons for older children and ask them to write a story about a season.

One teacher thought of another possibility: he wrote

poems about four different trees, characterizing the temperaments.

Oak
Despite the crackling light of the sky,
and despite the storm and peals of thunder,
whether my trunk is split by lightning,
or I am lashed by driving rain,
I stand here, the king of my realm,
strong and powerful,
I am the oak.

Birch
Here I am in my spring finery,
full of gaiety and white movement.
I do not know what boredom is,
for I am fond of everyone.
I'm pure and lovely, slender and strong.
Long live the spring, say I, the birch.

Lime
The summer sky is humming,
full of warmth and sweet colours.
Anyone who flees into my soft shadow,
enjoying my honey fragrance,
will find peace and sweetness here,
here in my lap, I am the lime tree.

Weeping willow
When the world is quiet at night,
I rustle my branches.

> The moon shines white, the air is fresh,
> my silvery leaves droop.
> I drift in thought, I am the willow.
> See, I weep.

In ancient Greece, a number of different language rhythms, or metres, were practised in the works of poets and dramatists. During the Renaissance these rhythms were incorporated into western European culture. Four of them were considered characteristic of the four temperaments:

- the *dactyl* (/ ⌣ ⌣) reveals the epic tendency of the melancholic temperament;
- the *anapest* (⌣ ⌣ /) reveals the approaching violence of the choleric temperament;
- the *iamb* (⌣ /) trips along with the sanguine temperament;
- the *trochee* (/ ⌣) is the metre appropriate for the phlegmatic temperament.

By way of example, the following lines from poems demonstrate the differences in these four metres:

The four metres

> This is the forest primeval,
> the murmuring pines and the hemlocks.
> (Longfellow, *Evangeline*)

I am monarch of all I survey ...
(Cowper, *Alexander Selkirk*)

As night drew on and, from the crest
of wooded knolls that ridged the west,
the sun, a snow-blown traveller, sank
from sight beneath the smothering bank.
(Whittier, *Snow-Bound*)

Tell me not in mournful numbers
life is but an empty dream,
for the soul is dead that slumbers ...
(Longfellow, *Psalm of Life*)

Every class in a Steiner school develops a special theme around which stories are told. In the first class, these could be fairy tales which are recounted aloud to the children through the year. Most are intended for all children, but on the basis of our observations it would be possible to choose a special story where the content related specially to a particular type of child.

For a choleric child, the Grimm's tale *Iron Hans* can be particularly appropriate: the caged strength of the giant can be released when it is used in the service of mankind. Jeanna Oterdahl's story of "The Swan Prince" in the anthology, *The Easter Story Book,* also has this moral quality.

For a melancholic child, it is good to hear how he may have the courage to step out of himself and approach other people, and to conquer himself. This quality can be found in Grimm's *The House in the Forest* or in *The Spindle, the Shuttle and the Needle*.

A sanguine child can learn from the repeated patterns in *Snow White* and *Faithful John*. It is possible to live more by luck than judgment, but to become truly "grounded," it is necessary to do more.

Finally, we can try to wake up a phlegmatic child with stories which contain exciting and unexpected events. Perhaps *The Drummer* or *King Thrushbeard* may arouse their interest. Time will tell. Another possibility is to tell a story in a deliberately melancholic way, and then have it retold the next day by a sanguine child; or a story that has been told in a choleric way could be retold by a phlegmatic child.

I am quite aware that this summary is by no means complete. However, in every subject the teacher will notice that children react differently to the lessons. Their preference for particular aspects of the lesson is revealed in their written work, their oral accounts, in class discussions and in their illustrations. In itself, this is very natural, but if their reactions and the way in which they process the material is studied in the light of the temperaments, a clear structure may become visible after a while which may well coincide with earlier observations about their appearance, behaviour, voice and constitution.

This applies to the situation at school, but how can it be relevant to parents at home to help achieve a balanced temperament? Parents know their children more from the inside; their relationship to their children is very different from that of a class teacher. The fact that they know the child "from inside" is because the child lives, eats and sleeps in the parents' or guardians' house. As a result, the relationship is on a different plane from that with a teacher, namely, in the field of life forces. It is very noticeable that a child demonstrates preferences — sometimes very marked ones — in this aspect of its character. We will examine this in more detail in the next chapter.

– 17 –

Eating what's on the table

There is a small boy, sitting in his high chair at the breakfast table, eating what's in front of him. His father is also at the table, with a steaming cup of tea. He's reading the newspaper and is just about to go off to work. His small son has finished his bread, and looks up at his father hidden behind the paper. Then he starts to sing: "Little Miss Muffet, sat on a tuffet, eating her curds and whey ..." The father looks up. "Do you want something to eat?" The boy nods happily, "Yes." The things these familiar nursery rhymes are good for!

———— o Θ o ————

When this same little boy was given his vegetables, he wasn't very keen at first, and this went on for at least two years. Eating difficulties occur in the best families, but my own experience is that it all comes right in the end as long as parents do not turn it into a problem. If there is nothing else wrong with the child, it is best if the parents focus as little attention as possible on the fact that a growing child has a temporary like or dislike of certain foods.

For my children and myself, every day was a new day with new possibilities, and therefore there were vegetables on the table every day with an opportunity to try something different from the previous day. From the start we did have a rule that everyone was given a portion of everything on their plate, though it might only be a very little portion if you didn't like a particular food. In this way the boy gradually got over his dislike and he now eats everything. He continues to prefer certain meals, but that applies to everyone.

Where do these preferences come from? It's rather strange that in a family with several children who are all given the same food, there are these mysterious preferences from the very beginning. This seems so normal to us that we never think about it, as is expressed in the saying: "You can't argue about taste." However, there is also another dictum based on the puritanical Dutch approach: "You eat what's on the table." From an educational point of view, I still think this is a good rule.

And yet, the phenomenon of innate preferences is a very real thing. To take this into account in a child's education it is obvious that the person who prepares the meals should try and vary the meals as much as possible so that they comply both with the sound educational rule and with the inevitable preferences.

The digestion of food in our body is one of the most ordinary "miracles" in life. Normally we are not aware of it unless something goes wrong. It is unusual to see food as more than the fuel which keeps the engine running. Many foods show the energy they provide in calories or joules, because we know that eating too much or eating greasy food is not healthy. Outwardly it is possible to follow the process of digestion to a certain extent; digestion has been scientifically investigated and there are no secrets about what happens in the stomach and the intestines.

And yet there is a certain point where something happens: the totally destroyed substance of the food which has been taken in disappears, and reappears "from the void" on the other side in the growth of the body, which can again be witnessed. This invisible turning point is the great enigma in the process of nutrition. What is it in our daily bread that feeds us? According to Angelus Silesius, it is "the eternal word of God." The doctor may call it "activating the life forces," but this is just as difficult to comprehend as the phrase "building the etheric body." Just as our daily intake of food is generally no longer seen as a "miracle," most of us do not usually realize that the shape of our bodies, the various organs and the laws operating in them, are also essentially a miracle. How does the form come about, and why exactly one form and not another? What are the forces operating behind this outward shape? Surely, in view of the fact that the human body harbours a soul and a spirit, these must be powerful extrasensory forces.

Rudolf Steiner was himself able to observe these extrasensory formative forces. However, he always pointed out that the same potential to observe the extrasensory is present in us all. It can be stimulated to a greater or lesser extent by means of meditation. The important thing is that we wake up to the fact that the spirit is constantly operating in matter.

The effect of this world of formative forces can probably be observed in its purest form in plants: germination, the growth of the stem and leaf, the flowering, fruiting and decay. The rhythms of expansion and contraction can teach us how these formative forces affect matter and then let it go. It is as though the spirit is breathing in the material world.

Light gives us life — the cosmic light of the sun, the moon and the stars. This is more than the visible measurable light of celestial bodies. This cosmic light also helps to form our human figure, but what enters from the cosmos is also connected to the earth and earthly elements: to mineral substances, watery substances and that which is related to air and heat. Again the effect of these life-giving and formative forces of light can be observed most clearly in the plant kingdom.

In spiritual science the forces of light of the etheric world are divided into four etheric types, corresponding to the four elements and to the four separate parts of a plant:

— the earth element in the roots;
— the sap in the leaf;
— light and air in the flower;
— the element of heat in the fruit and seeds.

The first type of etheric life, the *life ether,* operates in the roots and serves in particular to establish the form of the plant. The *chemical ether* operates — according to chemical laws — in leaf and stem, where the metabolic process takes place. The chlorophyll in the leaves and the colour of the flowers reveal a relationship with light. This is the area of *light ether.* Finally, there would be no life without warmth. Therefore, the fruit and seeds ripen in the *warmth ether* in order to pass on life or ... to serve as food.

Just as we identified a relationship with the four temperaments in the four elements, this relationship of our temperament can be seen in the field of nutrition with regard to the four types of ether. In other words, just as our temperaments develop because a particular aspect is dominant, so certain foods develop because particular formative forces (etheric forces) are dominant. For example, in a cabbage the leaf principle is dominant: everything turns to leaf and there is no stem. In carrots it is the roots that are the most important for the purposes of food. There are different forces operating in carrots and cabbages, and these forces enter us when we nibble a juicy carrot. As parents and carers, we should to some extent take the effect of these forces into account when we feed our children. I will go into more detail below on this subject with regard to the temperaments.

This is one of the streams which helps the body to grow through the food we eat. Another stream enters us through the senses. What is the mood like during a meal? Is it merely a matter of good manners amongst civilized people to try and make sure that meals are as cheerful as possible? I don't think so. It is well known that food is digested more effectively when a meal is eaten in a harmonious atmosphere. Experience of daily life may also help to explain some of the things I said above which seemed rather incomprehensible.

Anyone who cooks a meal for children or adults, for a small or a large group, knows that it is very important how the food is prepared and the mood in which it is prepared, and in particular how it is served. "Anything done with love is done well," and this should be the guideline for preparing meals for a family. Someone who believes that food serves only for refuelling, will put a baby into the baby bouncer with a bottle of milk in its chubby hands. This means the mother is free to do something else. But a mother who holds her baby on her lap as he feeds, surrenders some of her own comfort and freedom. You certainly don't have to be an exaggeratedly fussy worrier to realize that it is much friendlier. A bottle-fed baby already loses some of the physical contact with its mother. It cannot be proved practically, but I am convinced that a child grows and thrives not only because it receives the right quantity of milk, but also — and to a significant extent — as a result of the right amount of attention and security.

One part of this attention is that a carer should look at the way in which a child — our child — responds to food: how does it eat, how much, how often? There are good and bad ways of eating and eating habits, but what is good and what is bad? These are moral concepts which do not appear to be applicable to the field of nutrition. We think that it is a bad habit for a child to eat too many sweets. But who is to decide how many is too many? Usually, parents and carers of children subscribe to a generally accepted norm, in moral terms and in terms of health and hygiene. The growing child must comply with these, and it is right that these norms exist.

And yet there is another aspect of this matter. As a parent it is possible to see this phenomenon separately and ask the question: Why does the child actually eat so many sweets, and why does one child eat sweets when another doesn't? Why does one person like sweet things more than another? There can be all sorts of reasons for these preferences and one of these is ... our temperament.

The following recommendations on food for different types of temperaments were given by Joop van Dam, who was a family doctor in Haarlem for many years and often dealt with questions about diet and nutrition. In the light of our discussion so far of the effect of the four types of ether, we can be sure that food crops are certainly not all one and the same.

As we were already on the subject of eating sweets, we will start with the sanguine child. This is a natural born "sweet tooth" who eats lots of sweets. Sugar is easy to digest and therefore appropriate for the sanguine temperament: his connection with his body does not go very deep and his soul is connected only temporarily and fleetingly to the things around him.

We can help him to get more firmly into his body by means of the food we give him. Foods which take a great deal of digestion are particularly suitable, such as wheat (in the form of bread, wheat flakes, semolina, macaroni), rye and other cereals, walnuts and almonds (as for example, in muesli). The roots and stems of plants are particularly suitable (carrots, beetroots, celeriac, celery) and plants with a contracting effect such as rhubarb, sauerkraut, purslane (sometimes known as continental parsley) and gherkins. Herbs also help to strengthen the metabolic process and heat the organism (parsley, marjoram, thyme and rosemary). However, hot spices like pepper, mustard and paprika are not very good for the sanguine child; indeed, this is generally true for any young child.

For the opposite temperament, the phlegmatic, there may also be a preference for sweet foods. But the most marked thing about these children is that they will eat anything and everything which looks vaguely edible. It is this tendency towards a lack of moderation and fussiness which we can tackle in the food we give him. Unlike a sanguine child, the phlegmatic child is very focused on the digestive process and therefore the guideline for this temperament is to limit the amount of food and particularly stimulate the element of heat, for example, with herbs such as thyme, coriander, aniseed, fennel and dill. Exotic fruits and citrus fruits (lemons, tropical fruit) and raw vegetables also help to wake up the rather naturally dreamy phlegmatic child. It is good to avoid sweet foods as much as possible and not give much porridge or soup and try to always give wholemeal bread. The general rule of providing variety and making meals interesting applies specially to phlegmatic children. In this case the nutrition in the meal is determined partly by the qualitative aspect rather than the quantitative aspect alone.

Measures which are adopted to try and stop a phlegmatic child stuffing himself have the opposite effect with a melancholic child, who may start to eat with more pleasure. This is necessary because a melancholic child usually has little appetite. It is best to give this child modest quantities; do not give too many different foods in one meal, but make the meal exciting to look at. The food should look attractive so that this naturally rather cold child feels warm just from looking.

Warmth is a key word in relating to a melancholic child, and this also applies to food. The warmest part of the plant is suitable for food — the flower and fruit which have had most sunlight. Tropical fruits, apples, grapes and a lot of fresh green vegetables can stimulate the digestion, which is usually rather slow. It is good to give children camomile tea or lime blossom tea to help them to sleep, and for breakfast you could give fried maize porridge with butter and sugar for a change, possibly adding some fruit juice.

While a melancholic child finds it difficult to fill the body with the warmth of his spiritual being (they often suffer from cold hands and feet), the choleric child glows from top to toe and is bursting with energy. When feeding this type of child we must make sure that we do not stimulate this fiery tendency even

further. We can help to harness their sudden outbursts
of temper by means of the food we give. The choleric
child's fire can be extinguished in the first place by
drinking large quantities; fruit juices which have a
contracting effect (cherry and lemon juice, sloe), soup
which is not too spicy, porridge, milk, yoghurt, fro-
mage frais and watery fruit (melon, cucumber, gherkins). Foods which help to join a person to the physical
body such as pulses, meat and eggs should be re-
stricted. Of the cereals, oats is the least suitable: it is
well known that it heats up horses, while the rye in rye
bread has a subduing effect. Moreover, oats have to be
chewed a lot.

Earlier we saw how every temperament has its own
characteristics which can easily become excessively
one-sided. We can try to counter this one-sidedness in
a child's general disposition so that they can grow up
with a wider range of potential. However, we should
look not only in terms of the child's spirit and soul, but
also in terms of the needs of the body. In this respect,
food play a part in our efforts.

– 18 –

Four children in the class

A teacher at a Steiner school in Holland was asked to describe four types of children in his class:

Hans

Hans is a live wire in the class and rarely remains sitting in his place. He can never sit still for a moment and always wants to be active. He is usually happy, often impatient, sometimes dissatisfied, for example, when something doesn't turn out as well as he has been imagining for a long time. The problem for Hans is that he is punished too often. The reason is this. Whenever something happens in the class which shouldn't happen, like a remark that should not be made, someone who is sitting out of line, or someone does something he shouldn't do, Hans immediately jumps up and starts sorting them all out. He is not even aware that he is the one who takes the least notice and often does things he shouldn't do.

Hans does not think much but always acts impulsively. His hands are continually busy with pieces of chalk or pieces of beeswax which he has found "somewhere." And he can make the most wonderful things, imaginative structures, ingenious constructions; there is no end to his imagination. Only in his direct response to others is he inexhaustible and his reactions to everything his teacher says are quite exhausting. Everything is an excuse for a joke, a pun, to talk back. When the teacher gives him a cross look or says something about it, he looks very guilty and will keep quiet for ninety seconds. But then everything is forgiven and forgotten and he starts all over again. Because of his endless ideas he sometimes finds it difficult to sleep, and because of his boundless energy he sometimes has a stitch in his side. He will hit out at anyone who gets in the way of his ideas and is often hit back. However, problems do not last very long and Hans is laughing again, full of mischief. His eyes sparkle and he is looking for another adventure.

Tom

Tom is plump and friendly, and always in a good mood. Everyone likes him and he visibly enjoys this. He likes to laugh and likes a joke but when he is sad he is intensely unhappy. Big tears run down his cheeks and half of the class will be ready to comfort him.

The episode with the marbles was typical of Tom. Some of the liveliest boys had discovered that Tom had a lot of beautiful big marbles, pearlies and fivers, and other treasures. They had whispered in Tom's ear that they would play for him, and Tom had confidently shared out his marbles, dreaming of all the winnings which would automatically roll into his marble bag. With his empty marble bag he looked on, as happy as a prince, but his face fell further and further when he discovered that the "borrowers" often lost their marbles, and even if they won something, they would at most give him the worst marbles and pocket the winnings. Heartbroken and in tears, he went to complain to the teacher about the wicked world.

Martin

Although most melancholics have a dominant introvert aspect, this is not the case with Martin. He likes to be the leader and does so almost as a matter of course. He is always involved in many things at the same time, though rarely with what his teacher would like. His melancholic side clearly reveals itself when he feels unjustly treated. He can become so intensely angry and resentful that he becomes completely isolated in his mood. He just stands there saying nothing, just being cross. Nothing will do, and a lot of "adult talking" is needed to show him that his teacher's admonishment was not entirely unjust. One of his favourite phrases is: "You're always picking on me."

Martin visibly enjoys beautiful stories and songs. He also has a very likeable side which can be moving. He was asked to write a story all on his own. Unlike most other children, he wrote a long story in several episodes about a horse that fell sick. Although the farmer looked after the horse well, it still became ill. Just when I thought that the faithful beast would breathe its last in the next episode, there was a reprieve: slowly but surely the horse got better. It was a story of sadness and utter misery, but also full of tender loving care.

Saskia

Saskia and Monika are bosom friends. No matter how far you put them apart, they always manage to talk. They quarrel just as much as they chatter. Love and hate alternate so quickly that I occasionally wonder in astonishment how the friendship can survive with so much quarrelling. They scratch and bite, hit each other and are manipulative with the arrangements they make with other girls to play, in all sorts of sophisticated female ways. In this respect Saskia is undoubtedly the leader. She thinks of every game and knows exactly what she wants. Monika is more easy-going and usually obeys, as long as she is not in a mood to argue.

Saskia is an only child, and is brought up single-handedly by her rather insecure mother. It is quite clear who is usually the boss at home. Saskia yells and stamps her foot when her mother doesn't let her go out to play where she wants. Sometimes she gets her own way in the end. This can lead to tension in class because Saskia's wishes do not always coincide with the teacher's. However, when she sees that he is really cross, she calms down a little, respects him, and usually adapts. In this case she accepts his authority.

In the name of all children, these four — sanguine Hans, phlegmatic Tom, melancholic Martin and choleric Saskia — ask for our attention and help, and above all, for a loving understanding of the "coat" which they have been given to wear, and which they would like to grow into so that it will be a good fit when they finally become adults.

– 19 –

In conclusion: an answer

"It's strange that you never really get to know anyone completely ... not even yourself."

We began with this puzzled remark of a child standing on the threshold of adulthood, as she discovers the mystery of being human. In due course I came across a statement by Rudolf Steiner *(The Four Temperaments)* which summarizes all my reflections:

> Anyone who tries to achieve true insight will find the way to others and discover that the solution of this mystery lies in our self and in our relationship with others.

One of the ways of dealing with this mystery is to study the temperaments, both our own and those of others. The mystery of our own humanity is solved when we inwardly work on our own behaviour in relation to others. We can learn to see and value the individual characteristics of another, whether child or adult. Spiritual science becomes the art of living, when we not only try to solve the mystery, but also find that it matters.

Bibliography

Gudrun Davy, Bons Voors *et al., Lifeways. Working with family questions,* Hawthorn Press, Stroud 1983.

Robert Goebel, *The Four Gospels,* Assen 1933.

Wil van Houwelingen-Harmsen, *Ieder kind zijn temperament,* Haarlem.

G.A. Lindeboom, *Geschiedenis van de medische wetenschap in Nederland,* Bussum 1972.

Rudolf Steiner, *Discussions with Teachers,* Steiner Press, Bristol 1992.

Rudolf Steiner, *The Four Temperaments,* Anthroposophic Press 1971.